"You are going to love this book. It's a book that will shape the way you see your faith, your joy, and your freedom. I've met a lot of people in jails, but I've met more who are imprisoned by fears. Rick doesn't just jingle a couple jailers' keys in front of us, he tosses us the whole ring and says we can be as free as we want to be. What I like most is that Rick hasn't given us a bunch of steps to enjoy freedom—he just gives us Jesus."

Bob Goff, author of *Love Does*

"If you are seeking true freedom in your walk with Christ, read *The Answer to Our Cry*. Rick McKinley has written a book that fearlessly engages questions of freedom and true relationship, and takes the reader on a journey to find the type of love in the Father, Son, and Spirit that allows us to live fully, love boldly, and fear nothing."

Mark Batterson, *New York Times* bestselling author of *The Circle Maker* and *The Grave Robber*

"In this book, Rick McKinley treats ancient Christian theological themes, especially communion with the Triune God and the freedom of a Christian. While not directly citing Augustine, Martin Luther, and John Owen, he nonetheless conveys the substance of their teaching and work in very accessible idiom and through personal stories and pastoral counsel. This is great practical theology."

Tim Keller, senior pastor of Redeemer Presbyterian Church, New York City

"Rick points the way not to a God who is about legalism and guilt but to a God who is about life and freedom and love and compassion—a God who hears our cry and wants to set us free. This is a beautiful book. I hope you like it as much as I did."

Shane Claiborne, activist and author

"Setting the captives free was Jesus's expectation for the church. But how can we if we are not free ourselves? *The Answer to Our Cry* directly confronts the core of the problem—our inability to fully receive God's love because of deep layers of fear within us. Rick gently, with his pastoral brilliance, points the reader to find freedom with kindness, clarity, and truth."

Gabe Lyons, founder of Q Ideas;
author of *The Next Christians*

THE
ANSWER
TO OUR CRY

THE ANSWER TO OUR CRY

FREEDOM TO LIVE FULLY, LOVE BOLDLY, AND FEAR NOTHING

RICK McKINLEY

FOREWORD BY SHANE CLAIBORNE

BakerBooks

a division of Baker Publishing Group
Grand Rapids, Michigan

© 2014 by Rick McKinley

Published by Baker Books
a division of Baker Publishing Group
P.O. Box 6287, Grand Rapids, MI 49516-6287
www.bakerbooks.com

Printed in the United States of America

Library of Congress Cataloging-in-Publication Data
McKinley, Rick.
    The answer to our cry : freedom to live fully, love boldly, and fear nothing /
    Rick McKinley.
        pages cm
    ISBN 978-0-8010-1557-1 (pbk.)
    1. Liberty—Religious aspects—Christianity. I. Title.
BT810.3.M355 2014
248.4—dc23   2014021977

Scripture quotations are from the Holy Bible, New International Version®. NIV®. Copyright © 1973, 1978, 1984, 2011 by Biblica, Inc.™ Used by permission of Zondervan. All rights reserved worldwide. www.zondervan.com

Author is represented by ChristopherFerebee.com, Attorney and Literary Agent.

14 15 16 17 18 19 20   7 6 5 4 3 2 1

In keeping with biblical principles of creation stewardship, Baker Publishing Group advocates the responsible use of our natural resources. As a member of the Green Press Initiative, our company uses recycled paper when possible. The text paper of this book is composed in part of post-consumer waste.

This book is dedicated to my friends the Shomans.

To Terry
My good friend who left us too soon
but now knows the fullness of freedom
in the love of the Father, Son, and Spirit.

And to Shari, Jesse, and Isaac
To walk through the valleys of life
together with friends
makes the journey glimmer
with a few more rays of hope.

CONTENTS

FOREWORD

I remember the first time I met Rick McKinley. I wasn't sure we'd have much in common. I'm a pacifist, and he looked like he could pass a fist. I wasn't sure he enjoyed my Catholic friends and wasn't sure I enjoyed his Calvinist friends. I had the sense he could put down a beer or two and I'd come across self-righteous if I didn't.

I can't tell you how wrong I was about brother Rick, except for the bit about putting down a beer.

We hit it off. I have cheered him on from the other side of the country, and he's done the same for me. Rick is humble. He has been like the dude behind the curtain in *The Wizard of Oz*, or like a conductor of an orchestra who goes unnoticed. He just wants you to see the magic and hear the music of what God is doing in his city and around the world, and he couldn't care less if you know who he is. He isn't interested in everyone knowing his name or in his church being a brand or franchise. He wants folks to know Jesus and find their place in God's symphony.

Rick has carefully crossed enemy lines in the culture wars and has called for a cease-fire on all fronts. He refuses to make a home on the Left or the Right but walks right through the political waters like Moses parting the Red Sea. He is familiar with the growing populace of folks who want Jesus without the church and who want to be spiritual but not religious, folks who want peace but aren't so interested in the Prince of Peace. But the God he invites you to know is different from the God you've found confusing or bipolar or out of touch. He has carefully earned the right and the street credit to speak with authority about God and love and all the good stuff he writes about here. And he's honest about his own hypocrisy and contradictions—as you read him you get the sense that the church is not meant to be a country club for saints but a place where broken people can fall in love with a beautiful God.

I guess you can tell I like this brother.

He corrects the shallowness that has come to character-ize much of Western Christianity, which is so often a mile long and an inch deep—where our fervor for evangelism has come at the cost of discipleship. Rick is not interested in just making believers but in forming disciples. He isn't interested in growing a megachurch if that means having a crowd of spectators watching a few performers. He wants to see lives transformed and a world transformed—whether that means he has twelve disciples or twelve thousand. He wants a Christianity that looks like Jesus again.

Rick knows that at the heart of the faith is discipleship, which means discipline. And that is what *The Answer to Our Cry* is about. Freedom means creating holy habits, surrounding ourselves with folks who make us better, and learning to control our desires. We are not as strong as we think we are—so that requires community and communion with God *and each other.*

Rick isn't scared to talk about sin—but he does it like a good pastor should. A lot of people who talk about sin leave you with the sense that God hates people. When Rick talks about sin, you realize that God hates sin because God loves people. Sin falls short of love, and it hurts people. God can't stand to watch us destroy ourselves and others. God wants us to be free. As you read Rick, you get the sense that the Good News really is good. Jesus came because God *so loved* the world, and he did not come to condemn the world but to save it. God loves us. We are worth saving. The world is worth saving.

Freedom is a nebulous thing. So many folks think they don't want God or religion because they want to be "free." But when our anger makes us punch things, when our greed makes us buy things, when our pride makes us hate things . . . we are not as free as we think we are. We are hostages of ourselves. Our desires control us, our possessions possess us, our egos tyrannize us. Rick points the way not to a God who is about legalism and guilt but to a God who is about life and freedom and love and compassion—a God who hears our cry and wants to set us free.

This is a beautiful book. I hope you like it as much as I did. Thanks, Rick. And thanks for letting me beat you that first time we arm wrestled. I've been working out though, so look out, brotha.

Shane Claiborne
Author, activist, and friend of Rick McKinley
www.thesimpleway.org

PREFACE

If God is good, live fully, love boldly, and fear nothing, because all is grace.

Freedom is an innate longing we all have. We desire freedom from sin, freedom to love, and freedom from our anxieties and fears.

Jesus promises that the gospel brings us freedom in all of its fullness, yet many of us never quite experience it. But if we truly believe God is as good as we hope he is, then we should live fully, love boldly, and fear nothing, because we are free from insecurity, selfishness, and self-protection.

I believe this freedom comes only when we are attracted to the communion of love between the Father, Son, and Spirit. This communion has always existed and is what gives us freedom through Jesus Christ, the Son. We are brought into this communion not as guests but as legitimate sons and daughters of God.

This freedom gives us an identity, a mission, and a security that break the chains of slavery and set us free to experience God and life in a way we have always hoped we would. When this freedom captures our hearts, we are free to live fully, love boldly, and fear nothing, because all is grace.

It is my desire that as you read this book, you'll see a beautifully accurate picture of what God's complete love is, how he shares it through the Father, Son, and Spirit, and how we are included in that love so that we can go and love others.

1

THE
CRY
FOR
FREEDOM

Freedom is not a word I would use to describe my own experience of following Jesus. It's not that I have never experienced it; I think I just get confused pretty easily. See, my vision of freedom looks more like perfection. I wouldn't need God or anyone else if I were truly free. I wouldn't sin or fail or hurt. I would be free. I would be thin, and handsome, and maybe taller.

So freedom gets twisted into the idea that I should get what I want. But that's not freedom.

What if the only way we experience freedom is by being invited into it? I know that sounds kind of weird, but I think that is how freedom works. We are all scrounging around trying to get free from this sin, that addiction, those feelings, that pain, yet despite our many attempts to fix ourselves, we are all still here—not free.

What if the freedom we are looking for exists only in a home that we have to be invited into? What if there is a relationship that is so beautiful and perfect that the experience of its presence would set us free to be who we most truly are?

That home does exist—it has for all eternity—and the Father, Son, and Spirit are inviting us to come into this house, shut the door on the things that enslave us, and take our place at their table. But before we get to the front door, we have to look at where we are right now.

All over the world, at this very minute, a cry echoes. It is a cry for freedom. It is whispered in prayers, screamed in protests, and expressed in tears. It comes as a written word, is sung by souls held captive, and is sweated for, bled for, and died for. We are designed to long for freedom, sometimes enough to die for it, but what does freedom really mean? Is true freedom really possible?

Very early in the book of Exodus, we hear this cry for freedom from the people of God. They have been in slavery for four hundred years under the oppressive reign of an Egyptian pharaoh. Their days consist of forced labor, making bricks in sweltering heat. They work under deplorable conditions, and they cry out to God.

And God hears them.

> The Israelites groaned in their slavery and cried out, and their cry for help because of their slavery went up to God. God heard their groaning and he remembered his covenant with Abraham, with Isaac and with Jacob. So God looked on the Israelites and was concerned about them. (Exod. 2:23–25)

God not only hears the cries of the Israelites but also responds to them.

> The LORD said, "I have indeed seen the misery of my people in Egypt. I have heard them crying out because of their slave

drivers, and I am concerned about their suffering. So I have come down to rescue them from the hand of the Egyptians and to bring them up out of that land into a good and spacious land, a land flowing with milk and honey—the home of the Canaanites, Hittites, Amorites, Perizzites, Hivites and Jebusites. And now the cry of the Israelites has reached me, and I have seen the way the Egyptians are oppressing them. So now, go. I am sending you to Pharaoh to bring my people the Israelites out of Egypt." (Exod. 3:7–10)

God sees oppression and hears the cries of his people and sends rescue. He sees the misery, he hears the cries, and he sends a deliverer. He is a good God. This pattern takes place throughout Scripture. God sees the misery of his people, many times a misery they caused by their own rebellion. He hears over and over their cries for freedom.

So he sends deliverers.

Then he sends judges to rule and rescue.

Then he sends kings and prophets.

And, finally, he sends his own Son to bring the freedom we all long for and need.

It is for freedom that Christ has set us free. (Gal. 5:1)

So what does that cry sound like to you? How do you cry out for freedom?

Freedom is something we know is implicitly right, and we want it. We are designed for it, but in a very real sense, we can't seem to obtain it, keep it, or actualize it for ourselves. Which is why the cry begins to form deep within us.

This is not the way it is supposed to be.

I am not the way I am supposed to be.

The thing about humans is that we were made for a very *particular* type of freedom. If we don't first understand that one principle and then pursue it, we will never experience true freedom at all.

Freedom Needs Form

Ellis Potter has written a great book called *Three Theories of Everything.* In it, he talks about our longing for freedom. He makes an important observation:

> Freedom and form is another pair of opposites that we see in the world. A good illustration is gravity. Gravity is one of the basic forms or structures of reality but it gives us certain freedom. If gravity was not here and I began to walk, I would float and spin and soon I would be dead. Form, or structure, is necessary. Let me give you an equation to express this idea.
>
> Total freedom = Death*

Potter explains that you could declare your freedom by choosing to jump off a building. But you would die, because freedom always comes with form and structure. In this case of jumping off a building, the form and structure is gravity. Total freedom—freedom that ignores structure—ends in death.

So let me ask you this: Would we know freedom if we had it? Could it be that the cry we hear throughout Scripture and read about in the news and that creeps up in our own souls

---

*Ellis Potter, *Three Theories of Everything* (Huemoz, Switzerland: Destinée, 2012), Kindle edition, loc. 444.

is coming from a world totally confused about what true freedom looks like?

In the exodus story, Pharaoh is free. *Technically*. The Israelites are his slaves, and he is their master. That makes him free, right? But if you read the story, you quickly realize that while Pharaoh may have the freedom to make decisions, he is far from free. He is afraid he may lose control over his slaves, which drives him into the stress and anxiety of figuring out how to keep them under control as his servants.

Pharaoh tries his hand at total freedom, freedom without form, but in order for him to be free, he has to become an oppressive, slave-owning tyrant who, in the end, loses everything and dies. That doesn't sound like freedom to me.

The same could be said of us. We reach out for freedom from something or someone, and, more often than not, we find ourselves further away from the freedom we desire.

A man has an affair to gain freedom from his marriage and gets found out.

Total freedom = Death

A kid decides to escape his parents' controlling rules, so he hits a meth pipe and four months later is living on the streets.

Total freedom = Death

A woman works a sixty-hour week so she can have the money and the career and the security that will give her financial freedom, and she wakes up one day to find out she doesn't even know her kids.

Total freedom = Death

A man puts on a religious mask so he doesn't have to be honest about his doubts, but he ends up isolated from real friendship.

Total freedom = Death

Adam had a beautiful utopian life with God in the Garden of Eden, enjoying creation's perfection and his beautiful wife, but he wanted to experience (his perceived) freedom from the gravity he called God. So he and his wife climbed to the top of that building, picked forbidden fruit, and jumped. They died, and we've been picking up the pieces ever since.

This is the story of humanity expressing itself countless times in any given moment of any given day. We desire total freedom, and we end up dead.

If it's true that total freedom equals death, then what form of freedom brings us life? What form of freedom do we innately desire?

Freedom with Form Is Life

The form that freedom takes in Scripture is *relationship* with God. This is the gravity that holds our lives together so that we can enjoy the life God has given us. We call this the gospel: the Good News that God hears our cry and sent his Son to give us freedom.

We might think about this saving story as a narrative that has five parts: creation, fall, redemption, restoration, and consummation.

- Creation: A good God created a good world in perfection so that we could enjoy him and everything he had made.

- Fall: Humankind fell away from this God, and the sin that happened in the garden led to spiritual and physical death. We all are alienated from God.

- Redemption: God did not leave us to our own despair. He came after us by sending his Son to live the life we should have lived, die the death we should have died, and bring about a new creation both in us and in the world.

- Restoration: This good God is currently restoring all things through Jesus and bringing about his new creation so that the world changes (and we change too). Pockets of new creation are breaking forth in the old creation, and new life is beginning to dawn.

- Consummation: One day God will bring his creation and us together into a new perfection. That is what he originally created in the Garden of Eden. All pain and suffering will be done away with because this good God is making everything new.

Creation, fall, redemption, restoration, and consummation. And it really is good news! However, that's not all there is.

God's nature and being are the *main text* of the story, and our experience of creation, fall, redemption, restoration, and consummation are the *subtext*. Without the main text, the subtext doesn't make much sense (or even exist, for that matter).

I believe the reason so many followers of Jesus are still crying out for freedom and still finding themselves bound up in slavery is because they don't understand the most important part of the story—the part where we discover who this good

God really is. The reason this is so important is because our freedom is dependent on it. If our freedom is dependent on form, then the form of our freedom is relationship with the good God of the Bible. We will never be free until we *experience* who this God is through an actual relationship with him.

Freedom comes from desiring God for *who* he actually is, not *what* he has done for us. When we focus on only what God has done for us, we don't relate to God for who he is. When that happens, we are dragged into a whole new kind of religious slavery.

Our freedom is predicated on our being in an actual relational union with the God of the gospel. This means we will have to look up from the subtext of what God has done for us and fall in love with the good God who is, well, everything. Being loved and *in love* with this God is the form that freedom requires to be experienced. We will never be free until we love God for who he really is.

Freedom in the Father, Son, and Spirit

If we could go back before the world began, before any part of creation had come into being, what would we find? The answer is God, but not just any God. God the Father was there, and the Son was there, and the Spirit was there. Father, Son, and Spirit—this is the Trinity, the "triune" of God.

They each are equal in deity and unique in their person, but they are entirely one. This doesn't readily make sense to the modern mind because we don't think in terms of relationships; we think in terms of entities. The postmodern mind has problems with this too, because we think a relationship is made up of two people who are independent of each other. (And if it's not, we think the relationship is codependent!)

But God is a relationship *within* himself. The Father and the Son live in perfect love, and the Spirit makes that love realized and beautiful. They are entirely unlimited and complete in their affection for one another. They don't need anything else. For God, freedom doesn't require relationship with us; but for us, our freedom necessitates a relationship with God.

This Triune God is entirely free in himself as Father, Son, and Spirit; they are happily united and fulfilled by their own communion within their own being. So why did they create the world? Why did they create you and me and flowers and dogs if they didn't need anything?

The answer is simple, and it reveals the entrance into freedom. They created everything, seen and unseen, so that we can share in their love, their beauty, and their life. They created us to share what they have. *That's just how good God is.*

The journey we are going on in this book is a journey into the freedom that comes from being united with the Father through the Son by the Spirit. We get in on this relationship only because we have been *invited* into it. And it is only because God is so good that we have been invited into it in the first place. When we meet him, we taste the freedom we were made for, because freedom is a by-product of living in his triune love.

The freedom that comes from being united to Jesus Christ the Son, loved by the Father, and filled with the Spirit has three specific characteristics. I would define true freedom as the ability to live fully, love boldly, and fear nothing, and if you want to know what that looks like in action, then you have to look at Jesus. He showed us what freedom truly is.

He *lived fully* a life that was the very essence of life, because he came from the Father, who is the giver of life.

He *loved boldly* a love that bled out on the cross for our freedom.

He *feared nothing*; no powers of earth could shake him, not kings, or armies, or Roman crosses, or tombs.

Jesus was free because he always has been free. United to his Father. Filled with the Spirit.

God went to extraordinary lengths so we could participate in this freedom.

So let me ask you again, What are you crying out for? Are you crying out for freedom from an addiction you can't shake? Are you bound up in credit card debt, is your marriage on the rocks, or do your kids seem to be wandering away from God? Is there one thing you can't seem to stop doing even though you know it is hurting you and others? Maybe you have a void in your faith so that, despite all you know about God, you can't believe he really loves you. Or maybe you are tired of running on the treadmill of life and realize you are not getting anywhere.

What is your cry?

You can experience the freedom that will put you on a journey to live fully, love boldly, and fear nothing, because all is grace inside the love of God, his Son, and the Spirit.

2

LIVE
FULLY

I have three sons. They are each unique, but in some ways, we are all very much alike. The chaos created by the four of us just sitting at a dinner table can be enormous. I would love to say they have great manners. They should by now—they are twenty-one, sixteen, and fourteen—but they don't. The conversation starts out serious. But then someone says something funny, we all laugh, and the snowball of jokes starts rolling. You can't stop it. I try—trust me, I really do—but I can't. I threaten them as I try to keep my laughter in check, but it's really hard to send a sixteen-year-old to his room for being hilarious at the dinner table.

The other day we were driving, and Zach was describing how he once ate water balloons. What?! The other guys were laughing at the story, but all I could think of was, "Hey! You can die from that!" That's when Bryce, my youngest, chimed in. "See, Dad, you're always thinking of ways we can die from all the fun things we want to do." Such profound insight from a fourteen-year-old. I suppose I should just hold the video camera as he jumps off the roof onto a trampoline so I can show the doctor exactly what happened when he breaks his leg!

When you are in high school, you are immortal. Life is so full of possibilities that you assume you will never die. As a parent, you know better. There is something to be learned from both perspectives. My boys are trying to capture life by living it to the full. I am trying to capture life by making sure it doesn't fall off the roof and crack its head open. Life is this precious, fragile, adrenaline-filled, moment-by-moment offer of possibility. It might be the possibility of excitement or of death; life is filled with both.

My day-to-day experience can be very different from that of my sons. It can be more like the slow leak of air bleeding out of a car tire. For example, there are so many things I want to do before I die, like skydiving. But then I am confronted with my fear of heights. I start wondering, Who packs the parachute? Will they do it right? I see videos on the internet of people whose chutes didn't open! I can't quite get up the nerve to leap. I know many people take a leap from a plane and nothing goes wrong, but it doesn't change the fact that I am scared to do it.

Or maybe life is more like being a boy at a junior high dance, where nine out of ten hug the wall for the entire night. Dancing might look fun, but we're terrified to have everyone watch us shake our thing on the dance floor. Instead, we hang out with our buddies and make fun of those who dance.

I want to live fully. I don't want my life to be stunted by fear or insecurity. I want to live the life God made me for.

When it comes to faith, most of us don't really live fully. We never pack the parachute. We hug the wall like the junior high boy. We keep it safe, don't take things too far, and if we ever do venture out, we are careful because people are watching. When we encounter someone who *does* seem to leap without fear and dance the dance of faith fully, we think they are faking it or we deem them "superspiritual" and write a small check to support their mission.

But us . . . ?

Are we really living fully?

God in a Box

I really like King David in the Bible. I think he was a guy who did a great job of getting away from the wall and dancing the dance. He lived fully—not perfectly, but fully.

There is an epic passage in the Old Testament where David is finally done running for his life from King Saul. He is not just crowned king—he is anointed king. David wants God to be in the middle of his life and also his kingdom.

In the time when David lived, the presence of God was deeply connected with the ark of the covenant. The ark was a chest layered with gold. It had gold rings on its sides and gold poles that went through the rings. On the top were two cherubim, and the glory of God resided between them. Inside the ark was a jar of manna (from when God fed his people daily in the wilderness), Aaron's staff (which had grown flowers to show that God had chosen Aaron's tribe to be priests), and the stone tablets of the covenant that God had given to

Moses. It was a sacred vessel that held within it the dynamic reality of who God is and was. Because David wants God to be at the center of everything, David wants the ark in the middle of his city.

So David pulls together thousands of his men to go and get the ark, which is in storage. There are about as many people with David as would show up for a professional basketball game, twenty-eight thousand or so, and David is throwing a huge party as he brings the ark to its rightful place, in the midst of God's people.

Then this happens.

Uzzah is a priest who is extremely familiar with the ark. He places it on a brand-new cart, which in that day was probably top-notch Philistine technology, and strategizes the most efficient way to get God to his destination. But the oxen stumble, and Uzzah puts out his hand to keep God (the ark) from spilling out all over the ground. Right there, God kills Uzzah. And as strange as it sounds, I'm happy about it.

Why? Why would God strike down Uzzah, and why am I happy about it?

The manna, Aaron's staff, and the tablets of the covenant had long ago ceased to be symbols that pointed to the dynamic reality of the living God. For Uzzah, they were nothing more than religious artifacts of days gone by. Somewhere along the line, the holiness of God, the dangerous nature of his love, and the awe-inspiring reality of his presence had ceased to be real for Uzzah. He was a keeper of a piece of religious history, not a mediator of the living God to God's people.

Uzzah ended up in a place of being self-reliant, not God-dependent. When we become self-reliant, we never live fully, because it is only when we become dependent on a relationship with God that life really becomes life for us.

As self-reliant people, we always have God in a box. That is where we like him. We get to decide how and when he comes out; we get to set the boundaries of our relationship with him. We get to decide which parts of his Bible we will believe and which parts we will ignore. We get to pick God up and set him in the places we want him and keep him out of the places we don't want him.

Are you self-reliant or God-dependent? Do you have God in a box?

God was explicit about how the ark should be moved and the fact that people must not touch it. (That's why it had poles! Think about it, Uzzah!) The Levites were supposed to carry it; there was no mention of carts. Seems like such a small thing, doesn't it? Is God just being petty? Self-reliant people might think so, but God-dependent people who live fully trust that God knows what he is doing. When we forget the reality of who God is, we forget to treat him with the reverence he deserves, and holy things lose their meaning for us.

I think there are a lot of Uzzahs hanging out around the church today. A lot of us are self-reliant. The holy things we have been given no longer point to the dynamic reality of the living God. As with Uzzah, they are simply religious artifacts. The Bible becomes a history book, the bread and wine are a ritual rather than a means of grace, and the living power of Jesus is reduced to a story that we learn in Sunday school and talk about at Christmas and Easter.

When that happens, we die.

We don't fall over on the ground dead like Uzzah, but we die. We die to the reality that the Father, Son, and Spirit are present and actively bringing about our transformation. They are here, now, changing us by the Spirit and shaping our world for God's glory. But we don't see it. For us, it's religious stuff we talk about on Sunday, and it never gets traction on the pavement of our souls.

I think the fact that God lets us die like that is a good thing too. Let's be honest. If it were up to us, we would all have God in a box of our choosing, riding around on the efficient carts we devise. We would have God serve our purposes and us, not the other way around. We would conform God to our image and not be conformed to his. Uzzah is the picture of the self-reliant religious person who goes through the motions but doesn't get in on the dynamic love of God. We will never be fully alive if we put God in a box.

David's Dance

Then there is David. After God kills Uzzah, David parks the ark on center court, and everyone quietly leaves the stadium and goes to their own home. Finally, he musters up the courage to give it another shot, but something is different.

> When those who were carrying the ark of the LORD had taken six steps, he sacrificed a bull and a fattened calf. Wearing a linen ephod, David was dancing before the LORD with all

his might, while he and all Israel were bringing up the ark of the LORD with shouts and the sound of trumpets. (2 Sam. 6:13–15)

"Those who were *carrying* the ark." David goes back to the book. He doesn't take God lightly. He gives up whatever self-reliance he has, and he takes God at his word. David relates to God on God's terms, not the other way around. And when he does, everyone lives. In fact, they do more than live; they dance. The king strips down and starts to dance.

David doesn't live life on the wall with the junior high boys; he's in the middle of the action. And it's messy, but it's amazing. David is self-forgetful. Standing before his God, he lives fully because he forgets himself. Dancing is one of those things that requires us all to be a little self-forgetful. If you muster the courage to dance, you will really feel alive, but you might look a bit ridiculous. Once you get out there on the floor and give it all you've got, you will feel alive . . . and maybe even a little humble.

As the ark enters the city, David is not the one riding up high as king. During this time, a king would come into his city with a great procession of horses and chariots and dancers going before him. In the midst of this great spectacle, the king would come in riding on some type of impressive chariot, with the whole place cheering wildly.

But not David.

David puts God as King in the center of the procession. David is dancing before him like a servant, and the party is rockin'! David is living fully. The procession is less efficient, is more unpredictable, and doesn't have David at the center of it, but it is freedom. And we know it's freedom because free people dance.

I wonder if that sounds like your experience of life. Are you dancing, or are you dead? Self-reliant or self-forgetful? Do you want to be the one who rides in as king, or are you grateful to be dancing before him? Are you high and lifted up, or do you reserve that position of honor for God?

Unashamed

There is one more character in the story, and that is Michal, David's wife and Saul's daughter. She is watching from a window and, frankly, is pretty embarrassed about how this whole thing is going down. She thinks David is humiliating himself in front of the entire kingdom, and she would know. Michal grew up as the daughter of the king and knows how a good and proper king should handle himself.

Michal is also self-centered. She does not even go down to the party. David is not acting the way she thinks he should, and the party wasn't planned the way she would have done it. And perhaps the biggest problem of all is that she isn't at the center of it. That ridiculous ark is at the center of everything.

So many of us are self-centered. We find it difficult to trust God with our lives because he doesn't seem to put our lives together the way we would. Self-centered people are judgmental because they start with themselves and judge how everyone else falls short of them.

Are you dancing with David or sitting on the sidelines with Michal?

When David comes home after the party, and after he's blessed every household in the kingdom with a great party gift, Michal is right there ready to critique David on his dancing.

> When David returned home to bless his household, Michal daughter of Saul came out to meet him and said, "How the king of Israel has distinguished himself today, going around half-naked in full view of the slave girls of his servants as any vulgar fellow would!"
>
> David said to Michal, "It was before the LORD, who chose me rather than your father or anyone from his house when he appointed me ruler over the LORD's people Israel—I will celebrate before the LORD. I will become even more undignified than this, and I will be humiliated in my own eyes. But by these slave girls you spoke of, I will be held in honor."
>
> And Michal daughter of Saul had no children to the day of her death. (2 Sam. 6:20–23)

God comes to town, and Michal misses the whole thing. She doesn't get in on it. She never really lives. Her eyes are not pointed at God. She sees only what other people are doing and thinks it is stupid. She is self-centered, and she ends up barren.

Those of us who are like Michal don't bear any fruit for God. We are not free because we are not fully alive and have no life to reproduce. If we step back and examine our faith, we would have to admit that we are more concerned about what other people think of us than we are about God. We are critical of how other people are dancing as we stand by the wall and judge them. We are insecure and embarrassed, and we miss God every time he comes to town. We are not fully alive.

The church is full of Michals. We find it easy to look out at the world around us and point out how wrong everything is. We point at each other too. As followers of Jesus, we separate from one another over some of the smallest things, like how the water should be used in baptism. Sprinkle it? Pour it? Immerse ourselves in it? Let's start a war over *that*! How about the music, or those people who lift their hands in worship? What about those young churches where the people have tattoos? What churches are hot right now? Which ones are lame? What do you think of that teacher? Did you read what that guy tweeted? We love controversy, and we relish our own opinions, but those things never bring life into the world.

As a pastor, I see this sort of thing all the time. People standing on the sidelines with Michal and deciding whether other churches are doing it right, teaching right, worshiping right, doing mission right. Then they spend enormous amounts of energy blogging about who's right, who's wrong, who's safe, who's generic, and who's dancing the wrong way or shouldn't be dancing at all.

But the truth is that if you peer into many of their lives, you won't find much fruit because self-centered people are barren people. You won't find love rising up in their hearts for broken people, and you won't find gentleness or kindness. In fact, they might despise people, just as Michal despised David. There's no fruit because self-centeredness demands that everyone live up to a false and almost perfect, human-defined standard. When we do that, we are not free.

But David . . .

David dances. He blesses. He has this white-hot love for God, and you can see it in the fact that he is fully alive. David wants God to be all that God is, out of the box and in the middle of everything. David is anchored to his relationship with God, and that is why David is free. Free people dance before their God because they are living fully.

At my church, Imago Dei, we love to dance, not in worship services per se, but we throw great parties during the year as a staff and with our leaders. The food is great, the music is pumping, and we celebrate the year that God has given us to live fully in his love. Most of us aren't very good at dancing. In fact, if you saw us, you would probably be mortified. A few people have some sweet moves, but the vast majority of us have zero moves. But we dance anyway. This life is a gift, and our God has given us the opportunity to live it fully with him in our midst. We think one of the best ways to express how we feel is to throw a great party and celebrate the gift of participating with him in his life and mission.

Who are you in your journey toward freedom?

Are you Uzzah? He places God in a box and dies. Is your God simply a historical figure who isn't present in any real way today? Do you treat the sacred things as artifacts of faith? Is the Bible living and active, or a dusty book of stories? Do you look at the table set with bread and wine and anticipate encountering the risen Christ, or are they just crackers and grape juice? Uzzah is self-reliant and dead to God. Are you dying like Uzzah?

Then there's Michal, barren, critical, and blind to what is really happening. She misses the whole point of life. God comes to town, and she never notices him. Do you have lots of opinions about how other people relate to God? Do you find love, joy, peace, patience, kindness, goodness, faithfulness, gentleness, and self-control growing in you? Are you becoming pregnant with them and giving birth to them? Or are you barren? Michal doesn't come close to living fully; she never really lives much at all. She ends her days with no ability to create life because there wasn't much life happening in her to begin with. Michal is self-centered and misses God.

Do you dance like David, who is self-forgetful? He is not embarrassed or ashamed. He is in love, and he throws a party for the God he loves that blesses all the people who show up. David lives fully because he is free. Are you living fully?

In the next few chapters, we'll unpack what it means to experience that kind of freedom. We'll peer into the love of the Trinity and try to see what David saw, discover what it means to be the beloved, and learn to embrace life with gratitude and generosity. My prayer is that we will come out on the other end with the freedom to dance like David, living life to the full.

GOD is LOVE

Have you ever noticed how much drama hits the social media feeds among Christians after the Oscars or Grammys? Normally, it revolves around one of the artists who receives the award and then thanks—who?—God, of course. Now, they may be completely sincere, or they may be using God as a token of luck, like a rabbit's foot, but either way, they feel compelled to thank God.

Then the comments start coming. How could they make that movie and then thank God? Are they really a Christian? That song was all about sex! The mistake is in equating the word *God* with something specific. But the truth is that most people use that word in totally generic ways. We shouldn't blame people or accuse them of hypocrisy. We should simply ask, "Which God?"

God has become such a generic word. Ask most people if they believe in God, and if they are not staunch atheists or agnostics, many will say yes. But what God? Who is God? Which god among the myriad of choices?

In Portland, Oregon, a decidedly progressive city known for being "spiritual but not religious," the word *God* means whatever the person using the term wants it to mean. I remember talking with Sam after church one Sunday. Sam kept going on and on about how he loved the church and was learning so much about God and that the service times worked out perfectly for him because he attended a Buddhist temple earlier in the morning on Sundays.

In a sea of religious pluralism, followers of Jesus need a clear understanding about who the God they claim to believe in really is.

When you hear the word *God*, what or who comes to mind? Your answer to that question may reveal the most important thing about you.

Scripture gives us a particular answer to the question of who God is, and though the word *Trinity* does not appear in the pages of the Bible, the reality of a God who is three in one is clear. The God of the Christian faith is the Triune God who is Father, Son, and Spirit. One God existing as three coequal persons. Three in one.

The Trinity is difficult to comprehend, so people come up with different ways of describing this God. He is like an egg: the shell, white, and yolk all equal one egg. These types of definitions can be somewhat helpful, but they may betray that something is wrong with how we are approaching this God who is Father, Son, and Spirit.

Is God a fixed subject that we can pick apart and dissect? Is he a singular force, a large entity that has particular traits such as being all-powerful and eternal? Or is he an eternal relationship? Is God a big blob of Godness, or is he a relationship between Father, Son, and Spirit?

If he is relationship and unity, then the reality of his very being should inform, transform, and shape how we think about God, talk about God, and respond to God. How we understand God shapes how we see the world.

Many of us see relationships as two people coexisting but remaining autonomous. You are you; I am me. Who or what I am doesn't depend on you. If we think that way, it probably stems from the fact that we see God that way. God exists as a divine entity, a force, a power, so to speak, but not as a relationship. But the Triune God of the Christian faith is a relationship.

Therefore, it stands to reason that the way the world is supposed to work is connected to the very nature and being of this Triune God who created the world. When the Father, Son, and Spirit created the sun, moon, stars, water, land, plants, and animals, they said, "It is good." But when they created Adam, one man in isolation, they said it was *not* good. With Adam, they said, "It is not good for the man to be alone" (Gen. 2:19).

If the world is made up of millions of independent structures that coexist in autonomous fashion, and if God is a divine power, who cares if Adam was alone? Many of us believe that God is all we need. If that's true, then Adam didn't need Eve, or anyone or anything else for that matter. He was fine.

Why wasn't it good that Adam was alone?

It was not good because God is a relationship within himself, and humans carry the image of a relational God. It was

47

not good for Adam to be alone because within the very being of God there is never a sense of aloneness.

Think about it. The Father is not a separate God who doesn't need the Son. The Son is not some autonomous deity who doesn't need the Father. In fact, neither of them would exist as Father and Son without the other. Before all of this creation that we are living in ever existed, God was Father, Son, and Spirit.

This means he wasn't some force or deity who decided to become a Father by creating a Son. He was never a nonrelational Almighty all alone. He has always been the Father giving life to the Son. The Son has always been the beloved of the Father giving glory to the Father. And the Spirit has always been communicating this love between them.

When God saw that Adam was alone, a structure within creation without a complementary relationship, God said, "Not good." Then he created Eve, woman, and it was good! And Adam? Adam said, "Oh yes, *this* is so much better." Why? Because we are made in the image of God, and God's image is an image of relationship. We are not static forces, because God is not a static force. The world is full of relationships because God is a relationship of communion between Father, Son, and Spirit.

Relationship is at the center of everything, which is why when Adam and Eve sinned against God, they died. They didn't die physically, at least not right away, but they died spiritually and they broke relationally.

Why couldn't they just go on as independent structures? God could do his thing, Adam could do his thing, and Eve could do her thing. What was the big deal? The big deal was that the sin in the garden was not just an immoral biting of the forbidden fruit. It *was* that, to be sure, but the deeper sin was that it was a breaking of divine relationship. Adam and Eve broke relationship with God, the God who is relationship within himself. And so they died because Adam could not exist without God in the same way the Son cannot exist without the Father.

We are not independent structures. We are deeply relational people who are dependent on our relationships to be who we are. We are dependent on one another, but most importantly, we are dependent on the Father, Son, and Spirit.

Adam needed the Triune God, and he needed Eve. He needed the sun and moon and sea and this garden called Earth with which he was in relationship as he named and tended and lived. When he broke these relationships, his deep needs became fractured and he died.

What you think about God shapes everything else you think about. It shapes how you understand yourself and the world, your spouse and your job and your neighbor, and even the dirt beneath your feet. You are not alone. You are not independent. You are a person created in and for relationship.

God *Is* Love

One thing that's true of most people is that they're religious at their core. When I say "religious," I'm talking about the belief that God accepts people based on their behavior. We subconsciously believe God will like us and accept us because of what we do. It's true whether we're coming from a background of no church experience or a traditional religious experience. Those who have grown up in the church may think that if they exhibit certain religious behaviors, they will be accepted by God. Even the so-called nonreligious among us believe they can earn favor with God (he's called *karma*). How does the love of God break that religious framework and bring us into a dynamic relationship with him?

In John 3, Jesus is speaking with a man named Nicodemus, who is a religious leader. Jesus is blowing up all of Nicodemus's categories for who God is and what God is like. The verse I want to focus on is probably the most famous verse in the Bible. Some of you probably memorized it as a child.

> For God so loved the world that he gave his one and only Son, that whoever believes in him shall not perish but have eternal life. (John 3:16)

For God

The first two words are simply "*For God.*" What's your initial reading of the word *God*? Is he a judge who's distant and looking at your life, deciding if you're good or bad? Is he an absent father? Is he an impersonal force? Is he a policeman waiting for you to screw up so he can punish you? What is your image of God? That image drives your faith in a very particular direction. It drives you toward relationship, or it drives you toward religious performance. One gives life, and the other brings death.

When Jesus uses the word *God*, Scripture tells us that he's speaking in terms of a Triune God, meaning there is a Father, a Son, and a Spirit.

Jesus performed many other signs in the presence of his disciples, which are not recorded in this book. But these are written that you may believe that Jesus is the Messiah, the Son of God, and that by believing you may have life in his name. (John 20:30–31)

John ends his Gospel by saying exactly what he wants us to understand: Jesus is the Messiah, which means "Spirit-anointed one, the Son of God," which assumes that God is the Father of the Son.

The God Jesus reveals to us has been in relationship as Father, Son, and Spirit, in complete oneness, for all eternity. Before time began—before creation came to be—God was in a relationship of love. Father, Son, and Spirit are devoted to one another and glorify one another. They're in a beautiful relationship, and relationship always destroys destructive religion.

When we think of the word *God*, if we don't think relationship, then something is wrong with our theology. God is a relational God.

So Loved the World

And then God loves. "For God *so loved* . . ."

God *is* love and also *loves*, which means the very being of God radiates out from himself. Love is the core of his essence. That doesn't mean he's only love. He's more than love, but he's not less than love. Many people are afraid to announce to the world that God loves them because they're afraid they're going to somehow reduce the fact that God also judges, that he hates sin, and that he can show wrath. But rather than reduce God's love to something less than what it is, why not understand all these other things—God's holiness, justice, and yes, even punishment—in relationship to God's love?

God is jealous, and he can judge. He is truthful, and he gets angry. But all of that happens within the context of his being—his essence—which is love. He judges because he loves. He gets angry because he loves, just as we would if someone or something we loved was being ruined. If we read the Bible and come to the conclusion that we can't announce to the world that God loves them, then we're reading it wrong.

This God loves, and he loves the world.

After God created the world, he didn't back off. He didn't throw in all the ingredients and disappear. He created on days one through six and said, "That's good." And then he sustained his creation and is sustaining it even at this very moment. Creation comes from him, from his love, and is a testament to that love.

We were created to be included in his love. He didn't create humans and then say, "Now they can do good deeds to earn their way to my favor." That's not his intent. His intent is love.

Some of us think of God's love as a ladder. At the top rungs of the ladder there is real intimacy with God, but we spend most of our lives down at the bottom of the ladder deciding how far up we want to go. How seriously do we want to take God? Most of us climb up just high enough to believe we're safe but not enough to really taste God's love. We go just far enough to perpetuate our perverted and distorted views of God, but we never go high enough to have them changed. And *we're* in control—*we'll* decide how far up the ladder we go or how low we stay.

That's a bad picture. The truth looks more like a circle around your life. Everything that you've done, everything that has happened, and everything that is going to be is encompassed in a circle, which is God's love. God's love encompasses everything around you. It is not only the good things you do that end up in that circle. Every act of rebellion, every act of sin, every chance you get to run away from God also takes place within the circle of God's love for you.

Can you imagine a young child waking up and deciding if he's going to let his parents love him? "Maybe today I'll climb the ladder of mom's love." Children may be displeasing at times. They may be frustrating, and they may kick and throw fits and make a mess, but it all happens within the circle of their parents' love. If we, being sinful people, can love our children even when they are naughty, how much more must this Triune God love us, even with our most grievous sins?

Hearing that, some of you might say, "Well, Rick, this is an amazing sales pitch, but how do I know that God truly loves like this? I loved someone, and I trusted that love, and it broke. And then I trusted it again, and it broke again. Why would I trust this love from God?"

God's love is not the kind of broken love we've experienced on earth. His love is an entirely different sort of love. God made sure that his declaration of love for his world—for you—was rooted in historical reality.

He Gave His One and Only Son

"For God so loved the world that *he gave his one and only Son . . .*"

There was a man named Jesus Christ, who took on our flesh, lived the life we couldn't live in relationship to the Father, died the death we should have died, conquered death, and rose again to save us.

God so loved the world that he *gave*. This is the core of our story. It's not the announcement of an idea; it's the reality that Jesus Christ is the crucified and risen revealer of the Father's love for us. If we ever doubt it, we come back to this reality. This is a love that's not just spoken but also acted upon. The God who is love has come after us.

Whoever Believes in Him Shall Not Perish

"For God so loved the world that he gave his one and only Son, that *whoever believes in him shall not perish* . . ."

It's an open invitation. God creates us in complete freedom. He doesn't graft us into his deity, because we're not the Creator; we're the creation. He gives us complete freedom to choose to love him because the very definition of love is freedom. You never read a romance novel or watch a romantic movie in which one of the people *has* to love the other person, or they're forced into the relationship, or their brain is sort of hypnotized into loving the other person. It's the freedom of love that makes you know it's truly love.

God gives us absolute freedom so that we can be the "whoever." If we don't want this God, we are free to run away. He allows us, within the circle of his love, to run as far away as we can.

God risked our making poor choices so that he could make sure love is free. Love is freedom. In *his* freedom, he gave a

Son. And in *our* freedom, we're invited to trust in that Son. When we don't, we perish. We become less human. The further we run from God, the less we are like him. We are selfish instead of selfless. We are greedy instead of generous. We are vengeful instead of forgiving. And pretty soon there's nothing left of the imago Dei—the image of God—and we perish; we're separated from him. But if we turn to him, we can experience God's love and realize he made us to be loved by him.

But Have Eternal Life

"For God so loved the world that he gave his one and only Son, that whoever believes in him shall not perish *but have eternal life.*"

What does eternal life mean? In John 17, Jesus defines it as he is preparing to go to the cross. He prays:

> Father, the hour has come. Glorify your Son, that your Son may glorify you. For you granted him authority over all people that he might give eternal life to all those you have given him. Now this is eternal life: that they know you, the only true God, and Jesus Christ, whom you have sent. (vv. 1–3)

Eternal life is to be included in this relationship of love that has existed for all eternity. It's to be brought in by Jesus, through the Spirit, to the love the Father has for the Son. To taste and to drink that love, to turn around and be in the middle of that love, is eternal life. It's abundant. It's unending. It's what we were made for. It's beautiful. We don't want it to end, because it just keeps getting better.

The Faces of Love

To really experience this rich, multifaceted love, we need to know some of its faces.

Extravagant

It's *extravagant*. Have you ever gotten a present that you thought was too much? Every Christmas we agree with my sister and my brother-in-law that we won't spend a lot of money on presents. But then they go above and beyond and spend five or six times what we agreed we'd spend. I don't feel good about that. I open up my gift and think, "Oh no! I got them a calendar, and they got us a deluxe panini grill!" Instead of receiving it as a token of their love, I say, "No, I'm going to pay you back for this! I'm going to buy you something bigger and better." Why can't we just receive what we're given and be thankful?

That's what we do with Jesus. "It's too much! It's too extravagant. It's ridiculous." This story of God's love is outlandish. It doesn't even make sense that the Second Person of the Trinity would take on flesh for *me*. And if we have a religious mind-set, then we say, "Okay, well, I'll take it right now, because I really don't have any other options. But ten years from now, you won't have to worry about me. I'll get my act together. I'll be worthy of this gift." That's not how we receive a gift. "Well, thank you for the panini maker, but I'm going to *build* one for you out of a single piece of metal that I smelted myself." That response is not relational. It's religion.

Can you imagine a four-year-old, on Christmas morning, opening up a gift and saying, "Mom! You shouldn't have done this. I can't take this! I'm so mad at you." They don't do that. What do they do? They climb on your lap and yell, "Yeah! This is the jackpot! This is the best!" They're so excited. Children have no trouble with extravagant gifts, do they? And Jesus says we have to become like them.

If you really want to get this kind of love into your head and into your heart and keep those two things connected, then you're going to have to become like a kid and just be stoked today that God loves you and that he's given his Son for you. You're the object of his extravagant love—live fully into it!

Dangerous

God's love is also *dangerous*. It's dangerous because it's a love that is white-hot with passion and fury and honesty and jealousy. It's not a love that is like the ladder on which we can keep our distance. This love draws us in, and as we're drawn in, we realize, "Man, there's a whole bunch of things in my life that aren't compatible with this love." Like unforgiveness in my heart toward others. Like the hurt I cause people. Like the things I run to for life, when they really just give me death. And the beauty of this love is that, as gentle as it is, it's also unrelenting. God is going to love us until we're formed into the image of his Son.

Safe

Some of us think, "Yeah, I don't want to get too close if it's dangerous." But don't worry. God's love is also *safe*. How can it be safe and dangerous at the same time? I don't know. I just know that it is, in the best way possible. It's sort of like Aslan in the Chronicles of Narnia. He's not a tame lion, but he's good. That's how God's love is. We are safe to be exactly who we are right now; he just loves us too much to leave us that way. Perhaps our protest against God's love being safe comes from the fact that we live in a world that is not safe. God's love is safe not in a way that removes all the worlds dangers but in a way that allows us to be deeply loved in the midst of those dangers, knowing that we are not alone, and the one who overcame this world is present with us in the midst of its brokenness. God's love creates safety so we are secure in the midst of an insecure world.

Unconditional

God's love is also *unconditional*. We come as we are today. Now, if you're a four-year-old, you're like, "Yes! Jackpot!" But if you're a "mature," religious person, you think, "Really? How can this be?" Most of us think that we might get one free pass, but then we have to get our act together, as if God is saying, "I'll give you three years of unconditional love. How's that sound? And then you get your life in order and we'll have a relationship."

That's not how it works. His love is unconditional, and that's what draws us into its safety. It will never be more or less unconditional than it is today. Ever. God loves us just as we are. Before we repented, before we confessed, before we believed, before we ever picked up a Bible or had an idea about God, he died for us, out of love. He announced forgiveness. That's about as unconditional as it can get. And as God, he knows everything we've done and will do, and he still unconditionally loves us.

He's not interested in what image we project on the outside. He's interested in our souls—the actual state of who we are.

Unashamed

If God's love is unconditional, then it's also *unashamed*. God is not ashamed to be our Father.

Have you ever bought something that you were excited about but then discovered you had been ripped off? Every time you looked at it, you were reminded of what an idiot you were. The object lost value to you because you overpaid. We think that's how God feels about us. We feel like he must be ashamed to have purchased us. "He gave his Son for me? That's a bad deal! I'm not worth that." But God says, "I know what you're worth to me." When we have a religious mind-set, we do addition: "This plus this does not equal this, so you got ripped off." But when we have a grace mind-set, we don't think about worth through performance. We think about worth through relationship.

God's love is not about bad versus good; it's about lost versus found. Has my child run away? Or is he home? God is unashamed to call us sons and daughters. He takes our faces in his hands, and he is pleased that we are his children. That might be uncomfortable to us, but we need to learn to be safe there, because that's what we were made for.

Our Longing and His Passion

Finally, God's love is *our longing and his passion*.

We're looking for an extravagant love. We're looking for unconditional love, dangerous love, unashamed love. We're looking for a love that would give itself up for us. And every time we think we've found it, we're disappointed, because what we're longing for is *inside* the circle of God's love, not outside it. It's intimacy with Jesus. It's here; it's ready for us now, but will we receive it? This is what we've longed for, and in the goodness of God, he himself fills us.

God's love is our longing, but it's also his passion. He is passionate in his love for us. He moves toward us to the point of death because of his love for us. It is the greatest love story ever told. A metaphor that works its way all through Scripture is of the bride and groom. The groom comes after the bride, purifying her and setting her free by giving up his life for her. It is a romantic love story of a jealous God and a rebellious people.

The invitation to love boldly begins right here, when we realize that God is Father, Son, and Spirit. He is better than we could ever hope for. He loves us more than we could ever hope because he *is* love. He is more kind and generous than we could ever hope God would be. He includes us in his love with the Father through the Son and by the Spirit.

So what is our role in this relationship? We're simply made to enjoy this God as beloved sons and daughters.

4

BEING
THE
BELOVED

It's difficult for me to live in the bold love of God. I am so driven to produce. I want to make my own way and prove to the world that I am worth something. I want to do that with God too. Why can't I just receive the love of the Father, Son, and Spirit and live out of that love? Why can't I just belong to the Father in Jesus and enjoy that?

This becomes even more difficult for me when I am in a place of pain. It can be physical or emotional. Grief has the power to take me out. When things don't go the way I want them to and pain or loss knocks at the door of my life, the love of God seems really far away. My struggle seems relentless.

But God gave me a mentor many years ago to help me understand what it means to be a beloved son of God.

An Example of the Beloved

My daughter, Kaylee, is developmentally disabled and on the autism spectrum. Watching her try to cope with life is by far the hardest and most painful thing I have had to do as a father. To see her attempt relationships, not know how to navigate them, and then lose them is excruciating. My daughter is fairly high functioning, but that means she can feel all the emotions and loss but can't quite figure out how to fix things or why bad things keep happening.

I'm a fix-it guy. I'm pretty good at it too. I can discover problems, find solutions, and even motivate people to help fix the problems. I love to create ideas that are catalysts for people to jump in and change the world.

But I can't change Kaylee's world. I can't fix her disability. And I hate the fact that I can't. I've had many frank conversations with God about this. Sometimes I am arrogant enough to think I am kinder than God because I would not have allowed my daughter to suffer like this if I'd had the power to change her before she was born.

God uses Kaylee to mentor me. I don't enjoy admitting it, and I even hate the idea of it. I would never want you to get the impression that God goes around injuring people to teach us stuff about him. I don't think he does. But I do think that he takes the pain and suffering in the world and uses it to save us. That's the power of the God who is good and who is love as Father, Son, and Spirit.

My understanding of love has been pretty messed up. It keeps getting messed up too. Every time I think I get it figured out, I end up going back to the place where I get it all messed up again. I like to think of God's love in theological terms. I enjoy being able to think of God as the Triune lover, and I feel set free believing that he is good. But how do I experience that love?

We all want to live a great story. We want to be fully alive and to love boldly. Who do you want to become? What do you want to accomplish? Why have you been put here? How are you going to achieve your dreams?

If we look back at those questions, there is clearly nothing wrong with answering them, unless they become the tool we use to determine if we are fully alive. If we don't think we will be fully alive until we get everything accomplished, there is a good chance we will just walk through our days with life always out of reach.

That's where the Father uses Kaylee to teach me something that I keep missing. What if being fully alive doesn't depend on our becoming something spectacular or achieving something great? What if it starts with being loved? What if it ends with being loved?

Do you have all the degrees you want to have? Do you make the amount of money you want to make? Are you making enough of a mark on the world? Are you making the world a better place? Are your dreams becoming a reality? Do you have enough Twitter followers? When the answers to these questions determine whether we are fully alive, then we are on a dangerous path. We inevitably end up failing at some point.

I know this all too well because I live it. I want to change the world, I want to bless my city, I want to lose weight, I want to have perfect health, I want to travel the world, I want to write the greatest book, I want to lead the greatest church, and the list goes on and on and on. While none of the things I want to do is inherently bad—in fact, most of them are really good—such thinking can destroy my ability to be fully alive.

Kaylee has taught me that if being fully alive requires us to have answers to all of those questions, then my daughter will never be fully alive. Her mind doesn't work that way. She isn't afraid of failing in the same way I am. Her identity is not caught up in what she does in the same way mine is.

But do you know what she fears the most? She fears that no one will love her. She fears being unloved.

That is the same fear I have. It is the same fear you have. Except we can get sidetracked down a back alley called the street of dreams, where we spend enormous amounts of energy doing things that will make us stand out so that we can tell ourselves we are fully alive. But underneath all of that is just a person who is hoping that someone will love them for what they do. How much better it would be if we were just loved . . . period!

Kaylee teaches me that being fully alive looks entirely different than I thought it did. It is not about success, as we see it played out in the American dream. It isn't even about *doing* something. Being fully alive comes from a place of communion with God and others where we are safe to be who we are because we are loved. Being the beloved means we are set free by grace—to *be* loved.

This doesn't mean we won't do great things. Jesus said we would. We all want to live a great story, but we want to be loved for who we are. We want to be accepted even in our weaknesses, and we want a love that will help us overcome our weaknesses. Those are the stories we want to be a part of. And we want to destroy the bad guys and save the world in the process. But if those things don't come out of a place of knowing that we are loved, they get perverted and we begin to see them as the *reason* we are loved.

Most of us hold relationships loosely because they change and they may go away. We have places to go and things to do, and some of these relationships are, frankly, expendable. They will disappear, and we won't be brokenhearted about it.

In Kaylee's world, that is never the case. If an acquaintance unfriends her on social media, she is heartbroken. She will cry for hours, ask what she did wrong, and have absolutely no understanding of the situation. She may have pushed the person away, but she won't see it. She was just trying to love them.

There is no doubt that the way she clings to relationships is not always healthy for her. We can't seem to change her mind about it though. Kaylee assumes we are all here to be loved forever and ever. It's hard for my wife and me when she throws herself into relationships because we hate it when she gets hurt, and we know that the hurt is inevitable. Maybe it is right here that the Father uses her to mentor me the most. Kaylee has taught me about my own disability, which, ironically, comes from my abilities. There is disability in ability, and there is ability in disability.

Kaylee's greatest ability is her desire to be loved. Sometimes it's annoying—just ask her younger brothers. But she reminds me all the time that the point of being fully alive is not to live out our dreams independently of one another. Instead, the point of being fully alive is to be together around a table or by a fire. We are present for one another; we belong to one another. Each of us knows that we are beloved by the other, and there, in the center of that moment, is a young lady who is mentally around twelve years old and doesn't ever want that moment to end. What Kaylee longs for more than anything is the very thing we were all made for. She's just more honest about it.

We Are God's Beloved

Life in the Trinity looks like that. The Father loves the Son. The Son is the beloved. The Holy Spirit pours the Father's love into the heart of the Son. Then the Son does the unimaginable; he shares his own belovedness with us. We are the beloved sons and daughters of the Father because Jesus shared the Father's love with us. That's how he made our adoption possible.

It was costly. The cross is the intersection of all our failed attempts at living fully. It is that back alley of broken dreams, those failed attempts at finding love, the sinful off-ramps we take in our attempts to belong to someone who will find us lovable, respectable, and worthy. Jesus bore our disability (and Kaylee's too), but he also opened up the possibility that we can be named with a new name. *Beloved*.

Sometimes things go dark for me. I think about getting older, and I think about my daughter and wonder what will happen to her when I am gone. I know my sons will love her and care for her, but in those moments, I get angry with God. I want Kaylee to be whole, able to live on her own, and able to work and marry and have a family. I don't want her to be lonely.

When I begin this cycle of getting angry with God, I need Kaylee to mentor me again. Has my ability to work, marry, and have a family made me fully alive? The truth is yes, on some level. Yet in many ways, my expectations of *how* I want to do those things often cause me to miss out on the joy of *being* a part of them. I can be so focused on leading the church that I miss the joy of being with people and the amazing journey God has led us along. I so much want to be the best dad and teach my children all the right stuff and leave them with a legacy that I forget to just be *with* them. I want my marriage to thrive as we grow old together, but I can tackle the topic like someone balancing a checkbook instead of just loving my wife.

What Kaylee teaches me is that relationships are not economic. They are not transactional. We don't give to get. That's not a relationship; that's bartering. The relationships that make us fully alive are the ones in which we show up and we are loved, in which we understand our primary role is the beloved. Kaylee teaches me that the Father does not love me because I accomplished something. He loves me in my helplessness and in my continued disability of not loving but being selfish and sinful. It doesn't seem to matter how hard I try or how much I study or how smart I am. I keep forgetting this. The only way the cycle stops is when love breaks in and the Father names me his son, when I share in Jesus's identity as the beloved, when I drink of that love by the Spirit.

The sad truth is that many days I would rather be a servant than a son. It seems safer. I can *do* service instead of *be* loved. On those days, I am never much alive. I am not saying that love doesn't serve. But we serve best when we understand our belovedness. When we serve as the beloved, we are creating a new world with the Father and for the Father's pleasure. When we serve as servants, we are just doing what we are told.

Jesus told us we are the beloved. He told us with words and parables and stories. He told us by coming into the world and taking on our skin and hair and eyes, by walking in our dirt and living on our street. He told us by starting a revolution that he described as a tiny seed that grows into a beautiful tree. Then he told us again as he cried, "Father, forgive them!" on a cross, and he shouted it loud three days later when he burst forth from the dead. And he speaks it today into our hearts through his Spirit; he confirms that we are children of God, sons and daughters of the Father. We are the beloved.

Our belovedness is not something that takes away our pain and suffering. I think that's what I normally want. I get something deeper instead. I get a beautiful spiritual mentor who is wounded in her own right and who brings me to my knees in prayer, who helps me see my own belovedness. I learned that I am beloved by God by being a father to my own beloved daughter.

I remember holding Kaylee for the first time. She weighed only four pounds, seven ounces. My hand could practically wrap around her body. The doctors mentioned a few things that didn't seem quite right, but we never really had a diagnosis until she was seven. Even then there was uncertainty about what she had. After years of meeting with specialists and amazing educators, we are now faced with the fact that there is not much out there after high school for people like

Kaylee who are high functioning but disabled. We are in the midst of discovering what the Father has for her. On my worst days, I wonder if he has anything, but then I remember what she has taught me, and it all started that day I held her in my hands. She is the beloved of the Father.

She made me a father. I received that from her. She broke my heart in two and climbed right in and found her spot. She built a life right inside my heart. She will always be my beloved daughter, and she will continue to teach me about the ability of her disability.

If we stop for a minute and see the world through Kaylee's eyes, we may spend a lot more time soaking in the love of the Father, enjoying the friendship of the Son, and drinking in the Holy Spirit. We may quit acting like busy servants and become more playful and fully alive sons and daughters. We may never unfriend anyone ever again because we would see everyone through the lens of his or her own belovedness. We may wake up tomorrow hurting but aware that being fully alive is not the absence of pain—it is standing with another person in the midst of the pain.

Sometimes the ones the world has no place for are best equipped to show us what it is to live fully and to be truly loved.

5

A
GRATEFUL
REBEL

I learned an amazing lesson from my son Josh recently when his '81 Volvo wagon breathed its last and had to be put to rest. The car had lasted him a few years, but when we took it in for some repairs, we found out the amount of work needed would cost more than the car was worth. So my son sent out a tweet asking if anyone had a car they wanted to give away, and someone from our church offered him a great car for next to nothing.

This is where I learned my lesson. See, in my world, you don't ask for things when you have a need. You fix your problem yourself. If someone does try to help you, you politely say, "No thanks." But Josh has grown up around a culture of grace and sees God's care in everything. We were talking about it, and I asked him, "Don't you feel bad taking that car from him? Don't you feel guilty?"

Josh looked at me kind of puzzled. "I feel grateful for sure, but not guilty." That's when the bells went off in my head. Josh is better at receiving grace than I am. I twist people's gifts into something I have to earn or repay, but he can just receive them and be grateful.

So are you grateful or guilty?

I hope the story about my daughter in the previous chapter and now the story about my son will help you understand that our belovedness is not dependent upon our abilities. We don't work our way to love. We can experience the freedom of being fully alive today, right now, this minute.

How? It's actually pretty simple. And if I'm honest, it's pretty hard at the same time.

We've determined who God is. He is the Father who loves his Son, he is the Son who shares his belovedness with us, and he is the Holy Spirit who makes that belovedness real in our lives. God is three and one. He is a communion of love within himself because he is a relationship of Father, Son, and Spirit.

We are the beloved of the Father because Jesus has brought us into his communion with the Father. He shares with us from his own relationship with the Father, and he does it through the Holy Spirit. This is why the apostle Paul tells us in Romans 8:14–17,

> For those who are led by the Spirit of God are the children of God. The Spirit you received does not make you slaves, so that you live in fear again; rather, the Spirit you received brought about your adoption to sonship. And by him we cry, "*Abba*, Father." The Spirit himself testifies with our spirit that we are God's children. Now if we are children, then we are heirs—heirs of God and co-heirs with Christ, if indeed we share in his sufferings in order that we may also share in his glory.

We cry, "Abba!" Jesus gave us his own name for the Father. It is a term of endearment, of intimacy. "Abba" assumes closeness in relationship. We can call the God of the universe "our Father."

Christ shares all that belongs to him with us. This truth answers the core question of who we are. We are the beloved of the Father, co-heirs with Christ, and Spirit-adopted children of God.

Here is another way to say it: we are home.

The freedom to live life to the full is really about our core relationships. At the top of that list is our relationship with God. If we took a test, we would likely say that God is good and loving. But if we're being honest, we would have to admit that we often don't feel as if God even likes us. We see God as judgmental and not good. We start with the wrong image of God.

When we start there, we don't have freedom because we start with a lie about who God is. If that's the God we are living with, we never end up free or fully alive. We have to spend all our energy making ourselves acceptable to a God who looks down on us with condemnation. The result? Our lives become dingy with guilt and shame and fear. No wonder we don't share our faith with other people; no one wants to be miserable like we are, do they?

We have seen that God is a good and loving Father, and that the Son and the Spirit have made a way for us to be brought into God's own communion of love as his adopted children. And he really, really likes us! We are the beloved. We are free.

Being the beloved means the Father doesn't think of us as good or bad. Think about it. If you have kids, you wouldn't identify them as good or bad, would you? "This is my good daughter. That's my bad son. The verdict is out on this other little guy, but if his diapers are telling me anything, then he's leaning toward awful!" That is not the heart of the Father. He doesn't label us good or bad. He sees us as his beloved ones in Jesus. He knows whether we are lost or found, and he wants us home.

God made us so that we can belong to him and enjoy his love. That is what it means to be beloved. We can't earn his love, but we can receive it. It's a gift. Since God is a good God who exists in loving community within his very being, he doesn't need you and me, or even creation for that matter. But here we are.

Creation is a gift that overflows from the love of the Father, Son, and Spirit.

Redemption is a gift that overflows from the love of the Father, Son, and Spirit.

Our adoption into God's family is a gift that overflows from the love of the Father, Son, and Spirit.

Creation, redemption, adoption . . . it's all grace.

Returning Home

Jesus told a lot of stories during his time on earth about losing things and finding things. In fact, all of the stories in Luke 15 are about losing something that is important to someone, the mad rush to find it, and the celebration that happens once it is found. That story structure moves from a sheep, to a coin, to a son—the prodigal son.

The story of the prodigal son is one of the most famous of all the stories Jesus told. A father has two sons. One is younger and wild-eyed; the older one is stable and does what he is told. One day the younger son comes to the father with the most outlandish and hurtful request. He wants his inheritance immediately instead of after his father dies. He wants to be free from the father's home and do whatever he wants.

You can almost feel the tension in the room as the younger son essentially says that he wishes his father were dead. The father doesn't respond in the manner we think he would or even in a way that would be culturally acceptable at the time. He should have flown off the handle and disowned his son. However, he simply gives his son his share of the estate—exactly what his kid wants.

The son bolts out of his father's place with his suitcases packed and a party planned in his head. He heads for the city, having finally made it out of the trap of small-town living that he has always resented. When he hits the big city, it is all he could imagine. He has the cash to buy whatever his heart desires—women, liquor, pleasure, and the latest forms of first-century entertainment. I am sure there were camels involved. The party keeps hopping day after day. Night after night, he is the man on the town, and all his new buddies know it.

One day, when he is hung over in a stupor, he walks over to his bag of gold and sees that he has blown through the entire stash. All his father worked for his entire life is completely gone after a short time of wasteful, extravagant spending.

Reality starts setting in for the young man, and he goes out to look for work. He finds a job feeding pigs. Broke beyond anything he has ever experienced, he actually is willing and hoping to eat the pigs' slop—which wakes him up to just how far he has fallen.

He gets an idea. "Why don't I just go home and work for my dad? He treats his employees great, and at least I will have food to eat and a roof over my head." So the son begins the journey home.

The crowd that was listening to Jesus would know there was a huge confrontation coming. In that culture, fathers who had rebellious sons were supposed to stone them . . . not love them. They were supposed to teach the whole town a lesson about what happens when someone rebels against a family. But the father Jesus was talking about was so fundamentally different from the fathers everyone was imagining.

Jesus told the crowd that while the son is still a long way down the road, the father sees him. For this to happen, the father had to have been looking for him, hoping he would come home. When the father catches a glimpse of his son, he throws open the front door and goes running out to meet him. You would never see a respected patriarch like the father lifting his robe and running out in public, but that's what he did. He couldn't wait to see his son again.

The son is fearful, and he doesn't look anything like the wild-eyed kid who fled with the cash. His clothes are dirty and torn, and all the belongings he had taken with him have been hawked to pay the bills. It's just him now, humbled, broken, and embarrassed.

When the father and son finally meet, the son begins to give his dad a rehearsed speech. He is expecting to plead for forgiveness and beg for a job. But before the son can even finish a sentence, his dad does the unimaginable. He throws a royal gown over him and kisses him and tells his servants to throw the steaks on the grill because there is going to be a raging welcome-home party tonight. Why? Because the father's son was lost and has been found, he was dead but is now alive again!

The point that Jesus was making in the parables in Luke 15 is pretty simple: the Father rejoices in heaven when his beloved sons and daughters come home.

You are not good or bad at being the beloved. You simply are the beloved of the Father, whether lost or found. You are at home in your belovedness, or you are lost out in the world trying to find it somewhere else. Once you come home, the party starts. The wine flows, the feast begins, and the Father rejoices over *you*. Imagine the feeling you get in that moment. That is what it means to be free. God loves you simply because he loves you. Jesus made sure that the door to the Father's heart would never be shut on you. You are the beloved because God is love.

Gratitude

I think the key to the change in the prodigal son's heart was gratitude. Before he left and spent everything, he felt entitled and didn't care about his father's love. He just wanted what he wanted. But by the end of the story, something has changed.

After he has nothing left, he is willing and grateful to be his father's employee. He doesn't even feel worthy enough to be called his son again. Gratefulness and humility in our attitude toward the Father's love keep us joyfully at home. On the flip side, our ingratitude tells us there is a whole lot we are missing out on in the world. We don't appreciate all we have, so we go looking outside of God's goodness for something better.

In Romans 1, the apostle Paul shares the story of sin's devastation on the world, and it is interesting to see where he starts. Paul says it started and still continues through the power of ungratefulness. Sin's devastation begins when the beloved ones forget the Father and focus inward on themselves. They forget they are loved because they've turned inward to their own desires.

When we're ungrateful, we do one of two things. We run to religion, or we run to rebellion. Either way, we run away from the Father.

Why do we do that? It's a bit mind-blowing. Here we are, the beloved of the Father. We have been given identity as sons and daughters through Jesus. Yet, we still leave the house and forget about God and what he thinks about us. We leave God, and we leave the place of being the beloved.

I think we would like to change that, and there is a simple way to do it. We need to return to thankfulness.

I was listening to Ann Voskamp speak at a conference. She was talking about the power of thankfulness, the act of turning to God and giving thanks. Pretty simple but incredibly impactful! Ann's message about thankfulness hit me like a two-by-four, and I started thinking about Romans 1. The whole reason the fall occurred and sin continues, according to Paul, is that we don't acknowledge God or give him thanks.

> For although they knew God, they neither glorified him as God nor gave thanks to him, but their thinking became futile and their foolish hearts were darkened. (Rom. 1:21)

We become prodigals who run away from the Father. We waste our belovedness and get lost in rebellion or religion.

Running to Rebellion

Rebellion is one place that prodigals go. It seems that the path to pleasure, power, or pride will lead us to the place where we are fully alive. We are deceived into thinking that our worth will come from what we enjoy, accomplish, or create. We convince ourselves that life exists away from the Father and out from under his roof. We run from him to find life, but we eventually lose ourselves.

In John 3:19, Jesus talks of this peculiar reality to which we all seem to run: "This is the verdict: Light has come into the world, but people loved darkness instead of light because their deeds were evil." We would rather love darkness than be loved by the Light. Thankless people live in darkness.

Living fully is being satisfied with nothing less than the Father as he is revealed to us in the Son. We live fully when we allow his light to shine in our darkness, and we are guided by that light away from rebellion back to the place of peace in the Father's love.

Part of our work in remaining in the Father's love and living fully is simply offering thanks on a daily basis. It is not a hard thing for people who have realized how good the Father is and have been set free to be his beloved sons and daughters. Thankfulness allows us to enter the light of Jesus rather than getting lost in the darkness.

Running to Religion

Religion is the other place we run to when we forget to be grateful. Religion is even more dangerous to our hearts and our sense of belovedness than rebellion because religion is more deceptive. It looks good, but it takes life instead of giving it. Religion is more comfortable for us because we have some sense of control over it. The true darkness of religion is that it leads people to think they can control God rather than respond to him in thankfulness.

We believe that when we can self-correct our rebellion, then we will be acceptable to the Father. But if we correct our own standing as a prodigal, don't we have only ourselves to thank? Religious people are not thankful people. They are, more often than not, miserable people. There is no gratitude in religion.

If we believe that we live under a God who won't accept us until we're fixed, then we don't have a Father God. We have a judge. We don't have a Savior in Jesus who is all sufficient. We have a Jesus who died for us but wasn't quite able to bring us home. We don't have a Holy Spirit who is crying out from within our souls, reminding us that we are children of God. We have a Spirit who is absent or simply reminding us that we are not fixed yet. If we end up with this wrong perception of God, we are dying in the desert of religion.

Thankfulness is never the fruit of religion because religion is not relational. God is fully relational. That is why he has revealed himself as Father, Son, and Spirit. The Triune God invites us to be his beloved children.

It is also important to note that indebtedness is not thankfulness. Many religious people feel a sense of indebtedness to God, but they confuse it with thankfulness. As they read about Jesus dying on the cross, they are filled with the knowledge that they have a huge debt, but their attitudes never quite lead to thankfulness. Religious people are committed to paying back the debt. They believe that if they do the right things and don't do the wrong things, then they will pay back Jesus and fulfill their obligation.

Saying Thanks

Thankfulness is the language of friendship. It assumes a sense of being known by another person who has acted on our behalf, and we respond through the intimate language of gratitude. There is someone who is giving thanks, and there is someone who is receiving it.

The great invitation of the gospel is that all of us prodigals get to come home because we are the beloved of the Father. What are we to do after receiving such a powerful reception of grace? Saying thanks seems like a great place to start.

Living fully comes from the freedom of being loved in Christ by the Father through the Spirit, and as his sons and daughters, we receive it all with thankfulness. It is the radical infusion of God's grace through Jesus that sets us free from rebellion and religion and invites us into a life of thankfulness.

If you want to experience what it means to be the Father's beloved child, start with thanking him for being the good God he is, and watch as he transforms you into a grateful prodigal who celebrates being home.

6

A GENEROUS LIFE

I hate going to the doctor. I detest it. I get a little anxious, my blood pressure goes up, and I am always pretty sure they will find something terminal going on inside me. I think they call that hypochondria, but I just call it going to the doctor. At an appointment recently, I was telling the doctor how I don't like being in his office and how I hate that I can't control my blood pressure when I come in. On and on I was ranting about this and that.

He smiled at me, and he said that if I understood just a small fraction of what was going on in my body every single moment of the day, I would quit worrying about these things. He explained the blood and oxygen that were pumping through my body, the neurotransmitters that were sending signals, the cells that were reproducing and fighting off disease, and I began to see that with all of that happening at every moment of every day just to keep me alive, I had no business worrying about what might go wrong.

God has graciously made us walking miracles, and if we can realize how generous he has been in just giving us the gift of life, we may see life as a gift that we get to steward in his love rather than a possession we try to control through our own white-knuckled willpower.

Gratefulness and generosity go together. Grateful people tend to be generous people; the grace and love they have experienced and that make them thankful are the same grace and love that make them generous.

Generosity is always a touchy subject, especially in a culture of consumerism. Our minds go immediately to money because, for many of us, money is the thing that brings us the most security. The thought of giving away our money makes us fearful, not thankful. We don't want to lose our security. We think that when we have money, we'll finally live freely and live fully because we are secure; we'll have it all. Yet no matter how much wealth we attain, it's never enough.

Generosity is so much bigger than security. God's vision for the world is that it will be filled with people who have experienced the love of the Father, Son, and Spirit in a way that sets them free to live generous lives, not just to write checks to charity. Generosity is a countercultural idea that says, "Despite what everyone else thinks, I will dare to believe that I have enough." And enough doesn't always equate to money. We need to steward all our resources—tangible things like food and money, as well as things we can't necessarily touch, like love and grace.

We really can only live generous lives when we live in the

freedom of love. That is the place where we learn that nothing is earned, all is a gift, and we are free to lay it all down for the one who laid it all down for us. Grateful people are transformed because they have been touched by God's generosity—the incomprehensible, magnificent, outrageous generosity of a loving God.

The Father, Son, and Spirit do not live in an economy of scarcity. There is no lack. There is enough love, energy, life, and freedom within the context of the Godhead that they are never selfish. Because God is three persons, he is never self-centered. He is other-centered and self-giving. We are made to reflect that type of generous life back to God and to one another, but our sin has turned us inward, and when we look into ourselves, we never find enough.

But that is not the case with God. There is only abundance within him. There is enough, and there will always be enough. The cascading effect of abundance generously flows down to us, and we have the potential of being radically transformed by it.

Many of us are not free to live generous lives because somewhere in our broken world we learned that there may not be enough. We have to look out for ourselves. We live as though we're in need, scrounging around for our next meal when, in reality, we are the sons and daughters of a God who has everything we'll ever need.

If we live with a mind-set of scarcity, we convince ourselves that we have to hoard our lives. We exert so much effort trying to protect our time, our money, and our energy that it is impossible for us to be generous.

From Not Enough to More Than Enough

The power of being loved by this generous God is that our paradigms begin to shift. God is a generous God. The Father is not selfish with his love. He gives it to the Son, who isn't selfish with it either. He turns and gives it to us. The Spirit doesn't sit around wondering when he will get his share. He pours the love of the Father into our hearts. Generosity flows all around.

When generosity touches our lives, it sets us free. We begin to see that God is the source of life, his life is endless, and he has brought us into that life through the Son. Then our mind-set of scarcity disappears, and we are brought into the fullness of life.

What if we found life not in trying to get everything we want but in giving away everything we have? What if life is in generosity because God is a God of generosity? What if we were made to live fully when we live in his generosity?

Our lives find a deep and significant meaning when we mirror the God in whose image we were made. Freedom comes when that cascading love is poured into our hearts through the Spirit. We are convinced there is enough love for everyone. There is an endless supply of life for us in Jesus. When we give a piece of that life away, it gets replenished.

Second Corinthians 8:9 tells us, "For you know the grace of our Lord Jesus Christ, that though he was rich, yet for your sake he became poor, so that you through his poverty might become rich." It takes a radical infusion of grace to set someone free from living a self-protecting life. Jesus shares his wealth of life and love and relationship with the Father, but he does it by taking on our desert of poverty. He became poor, impoverished, stricken, beaten, and crucified. He gave us everything he had until he breathed his last on the cross, asking the Father to offer us forgiveness. Generosity was in his dying breath. How could he do that? He could do that because he knew that the Father's endless love, endless power, and endless life would overcome our poverty and raise him from the grave into a new life that can never die.

The grave is perhaps the darkest symbol of the desert of scarcity. The lifeless body that is buried in the ground has no capacity for generosity. There is nothing left in it to give to anyone. It is simply dead. While most people are not aware of it, we are living as the walking dead. We are halfway buried in selfishness and wondering why our endless quest to get more for ourselves is not producing in us the quality of life that our souls are deeply thirsting for.

Jesus exchanges our scarcity for his abundance. When we are at home in the Father's house, set free by the crucified and risen King, we are transferred into a world of abundance where there is enough for everyone. This kind of abundance unlocks the shackles of our greedy lives, allowing us to step out into a new way of living as beloved sons and daughters who have been given so much that the life of the Spirit begins to overflow into the lives of others through our generosity.

We won't be set free to be generous just by knowing about it. Generosity has to touch our lives. We are quick to forget the poverty and debt we were in before we knew God. We didn't have the resources in ourselves to offer much to anyone. We couldn't love others selflessly, because we were only in it for ourselves. We were helpless to fill up the empty accounts of love and life in our own hearts. That's where the generosity of God shows up. God gives us his Son, and the Son takes our bankrupt hearts and our debts of sin and pays them off by bearing the cross for us. Jesus literally gives us his life, and he does it to the Father's glory. The Father is glorified in the generosity of Jesus's love for us, and this love shows up in our lives through the Spirit (whom Jesus gives us as well).

My friend Steve has given his life to share the message of generosity. He describes his job as performing jailbreaks for people. He works with people of great wealth, and he shares with them a new vision of life. That vision is the freedom of generosity.

He told me a story of a man who had an abundance of wealth. Steve was talking to the man's daughter, who described the time her dad brought her adopted sister home. The little girl was adopted from overseas, and after an extensive adoption process, the day finally arrived when they could travel abroad and bring their new little girl home. When they arrived home to their ranch, her father picked the little girl up in his arms and walked her around the house. He showed the girl her bedroom and asked, "Did you know you had your own bedroom? Did you know you had so many toys?" He walked her outside. "Did you know you had a horse?" He walked her around every piece of their property, asking her all the time if she knew she had so much. The little girl was amazed that everything that was his was now hers as well.

As the older daughter told my friend Steve this story, her eyes welled up with tears as she said, "I thought to myself,

'That little girl did nothing to earn any of these things that her father had told her were hers, and neither did I.'"

That is what our Father has done for us. He has taken us out of a world of scarcity and adopted us as his own through Jesus. He happily shares with us all that is his in his house. Because we now live in a new world, nothing is earned and everything is given to us. That is the heart of the Father. Once we have this understanding, the question quickly moves from "How do I keep what is mine?" to "How can I share all that I have been given?"

Free to Be Generous

The people of God are set free to be generous people who live out the vision of generosity. That vision was given to us by the one who shared all he had with us. How does the abundance of God's grace create the freedom for us to live a generous life?

When we are on the receiving end of generosity, it changes us. I have been changed by the generosity of God and the generosity of others. When people made time for me when I was hurting or paid off debts I had, I experienced the radical power of generosity by being on the receiving end. Generosity makes grace tangible. Each time I experienced generosity, I was surprised. I didn't deserve it. No one had to make time for me, help me, or open up and share with me. They did it as a sacred act of generous love. That is the type of thing that changes the world.

How have you experienced the generosity of the Father, Son, and Spirit? Where has God placed people in your life to extend his generosity to you in tangible acts of grace and kindness that deeply met your needs?

Generosity has a prophetic edge to it. It makes us look up from the chaos, from our clamoring for what we can get for ourselves, and realize there is another path—the way of love. From opening our homes, to putting an extra chair at the table, to making space on our calendars, to quietly giving money to someone in need, each of these actions shows that the world is not a place where we are left to fend for ourselves. Instead, it is open to the generosity of God. It is a place where we are free to be generous. Imagine how these acts could change our neighborhoods. They do not have to be extravagant. Often the small acts are the ones that are the most powerful.

What if no one felt alone because people were generous enough to care when they were hurting? What if no one went through the heartache of loss alone because people made space to sit and listen and weep with them? What if there was an alternative community of people in this world who lived out of an economy of abundance because they had been brought into the wealth of the Father's loving care? What would that world look like, and how different is it from the one we live in now?

Generosity is paradoxical and, at its core, it is the basic teaching of Jesus. If we want to gain our life, we need to lose it. When we give ourselves away to another, we actually gain much more than we give. And we are free to do that because Jesus has freely given us himself.

Generosity involves giving ourselves to another person. That exchange between two people who bear the image of our generous God is filled with potential for transformation. At the intersection of those two lives, a bond is created when grace and love travel back and forth between them. Jesus binds two lives together for his glory. Both people are changed in that moment. It is in this place that we are free to be changed by the power of a generous God.

In this wilderness of a world that is scarce and barren, a gift of abundance will fuel our souls not only to survive the conditions of a broken world but also to thrive in them and to have enough left over for our neighbor.

Lavish grace creates a community of generous people who are free to love, bless, and heal the neighborhoods of our world in the name of Jesus. Even when the circumstances scream there is not enough, if Jesus is present, there will always be abundance. A generous life flows from the abundance of Christ.

7

LOVE
BOLDLY

Sometimes I wish I could replace the word *love* in Scripture with "be a nice person." Actually, I have. I haven't gone through and edited Scripture with a pen, but I have my own internal editing system that filters hard passages and spits them out in a way that I find more acceptable, and I don't think I am alone.

"Love your enemies" becomes "tolerate people you don't like."

"Love your neighbor" becomes "smile and wave to them if you are in the front yard and they happen to drive by."

Perhaps the worst one is "Love God with all your heart, mind, soul, and strength," which gets translated into "try not to sin and make God mad."

These changes don't happen in an obvious manner; they happen over time, and eventually we just become comfortable with the edits we make to the love of God. But following this twisted version of the Bible does not lead us to freedom. It doesn't create the bold love with which Jesus has loved us. It creates a group of nice people who are really not all that loving.

This is not the kind of freedom we were made for. The Father, Son, and Spirit were aiming for a whole lot more than *nice*. They were aiming at creating people who could live a life of freedom and love with courage and boldness. That freedom is available to us right now, but something pretty massive is needed to remove our internal editing buttons and create a new kind of boldness that doesn't seem to come naturally.

The Grace to Love

We need a substantial infusion of grace to remove the chains of our self-protection so that we have the freedom to love both God and others. The editing button is a pretty powerful internal mechanism. I find it useful in protecting myself from having to deal with people or when I want to stay in my comfort zone. It allows my world to dwell within the grasp of my control. There isn't much that could motivate me to give it up, and even if I wanted to, I don't have the power on my own to do so.

That's where the grace of our good God shows up, because the very nature of God is other-centered. The Father's love is focused on the Son, the Son's love is focused on the Father, and the Spirit is moving to express that love. The Trinity is a communion of other-centeredness. That is so different from who I am. I am self-centered. I replace a love for God with a love for myself. And I can't change this on my own.

Showing love to others is not God's idea of how to make the world a nicer place. It is the foundation of his very nature. There is diversity within the Triune God, which means that before God created anything, there was another, someone within himself, to love. He was enjoying the freedom of a love that has another person as the object of that love. The Father freely loves the Son, and the Son freely loves the Father. There is diversity because the Father is not the Son, and the Son is not the Father. To add more diversity into the mix, the Spirit expresses the love between the Father and the Son.

Yet, there is also unity because the Son is not the Son without the Father, and the Father is not the Father without the Son, and their love is not communicated without the Spirit, who unites them in this love.

Michael Reeves, in his excellent book titled *Delighting in the Trinity*, explains the Spirit's work this way: "The Spirit stirs up the delight of the Father in the Son and the delight of the Son in the Father, inflaming their love and so binding them together in 'the fellowship of the Holy Spirit' (2 Cor 13:14)."* It is this love that has always existed even before the universe began. God boldly expresses this divine love in the communion of Father, Son, and Spirit.

We are powerfully set free from the love of self and the chains of self-protection because this good and loving God focuses his love on others—on us—in grace. As an act of divine love and goodness, God has chosen to love us. It is here, in God's choice to love us, that an infusion of grace takes place. There is nothing we can do to make God love us. He loves us because he is good. When we clearly don't deserve that kind of love, he loves us anyway with boldness. Jesus's

*Michael Reeves, *Delighting in the Trinity: An Introduction to the Christian Faith* (Downers Grove, IL: InterVarsity, 2012), 29.

love is a bold love, a love that caused him to lay down his life for us. That is the greatest love there is.

Grace is not something the Father needed to offer to the Son. The Son was not a selfish prodigal. For all eternity he has been a devoted Son who loves being loved by the Father and bringing him glory. No, grace was something created out of love so that people who don't deserve to be loved are loved. Grace was created out of love so that people who are chained up in lives of self-centeredness can be set free by the one who laid down his life for our freedom. Grace was created out of love so that we could be rescued from being nice people and become people who love the world the way Jesus does. Grace is something God created so that we could be brought into his love. Grace made sure that, as different as we are from God, the Spirit could unite us to the Father through the Son. That is love.

That love opens the door for us to begin to embrace others. As partakers of this divine love, we not only receive it for ourselves but also give it to others. We have a sacred trust that God will fill us with his love so that we can be free to offer it to others and express it back to God. Our love by itself is always insufficient, but his love is all-sufficient. As we partake of it and express it, we are not simply offering someone our own love but the love that has been given to us. We offer the love of the Father through the Son by the Spirit.

Loving Like Jesus

If grace sets us free from the love of self, then how do we begin to love like Jesus? First, it is important to talk about who it is we are free to love. The first object of our love is God. We are free to love the Triune God. But how? Do we love the Father? Do we love the Son? What about the Spirit? How does all of this work?

The simplest answer is this: we love the Triune God in the face of Jesus. All of the grace we have been given has been given to us in Jesus. The apostle Paul said it this way:

> For what we preach is not ourselves, but Jesus Christ as Lord, and ourselves as your servants for Jesus' sake. For God, who said, "Let light shine out of darkness," made his light shine in our hearts to give us the light of the knowledge of God's glory displayed in the face of Christ. (2 Cor. 4:5–6)

We are not brought into God's love by studying abstract thoughts about God. God comes to us in the person of Jesus so that the knowledge of God's glory can shine in our hearts. Jesus is the first *other* we have been set free to love with boldness. When we love Jesus, we love the Father, Son, and Spirit, because the God whom Jesus reveals is always the Triune God.

When we love Jesus, we are responding, not initiating. This is something we often miss. The infusion of grace that we receive is that God loved us first! We love because he first loved us, not the other way around. We have been loved by the Father in relationship to Jesus, and the Holy Spirit makes that love known to us. We respond by loving the Father in the face of Jesus by the power of the Holy Spirit. As we see in the following diagram, this is what communion looks like.

We are free to love Jesus and, in turn, to boldly love other people. Jesus tells us in Matthew's Gospel what this means.

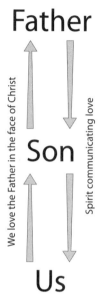

Father

We love the Father in the face of Christ

Spirit communicating love

Son

Us

Then the King will say to those on his right, "Come, you who are blessed by my Father; take your inheritance, the kingdom prepared for you since the creation of the world. For I was hungry and you gave me something to eat, I was thirsty and you gave me something to drink, I was a stranger and you invited me in, I needed clothes and you clothed me, I was sick and you looked after me, I was in prison and you came to visit me."

Then the righteous will answer him, "Lord, when did we see you hungry and feed you, or thirsty and give you something to drink? When did we see you a stranger and invite you in, or needing clothes and clothe you? When did we see you sick or in prison and go to visit you?"

The King will reply, "Truly I tell you, whatever you did for one of the least of these brothers and sisters of mine, you did for me." (25:34–40)

In this story, we get the who and the how of bold love. Who is it that we love? We love Jesus the King. How do we love him? By loving the thirsty, the naked, the sick, and the imprisoned with bold and tangible love. We love Jesus in the face of another person.

Mother Teresa was asked how she sustained her work of loving those ravaged with leprosy and living in abject poverty. How was it that day in and day out she mustered the courage and the perseverance to keep loving and serving those whom the world had forgotten? As the story goes, she responded, "We do it to Jesus."

She served Jesus by serving a woman with leprosy. She loved Jesus and the woman at the same time. Her years of working with suffering people had taught her what Jesus tells us in this passage. We will find the face of Jesus in the face of another person. When that happens, we are free to love, and that love will be unstoppable.

I have a friend named Sarah who takes public transportation on purpose. Even though Sarah owns a car, she intentionally takes a bus or a train just so she can find Jesus in the faces of others. One time when she was riding, a single mom and her five children were on the train. One of the children ran up to her and jumped on her lap. Sarah was taken aback at first. Then the child settled into her arms, and the mother gave her a smile that assured her she approved. The family was from Somalia and had moved to the US as refugees. When the train came to the woman's stop, Sarah exited the train with them. It wasn't her stop, but she knew it was where she needed to get off.

She helped the mother and her children back to their apartment. As she walked in, she realized she had never seen poverty like this before. There was no food in the house; the kids had been living on stale bread and ketchup. They had few clothes and fewer belongings. Sarah was filled with love for them. She understood that their situation was going unnoticed by the people around them. They were invisible.

But not to Sarah. Sarah was filled with a boldness to love them and keep loving them. Sarah knew what it was like to be invisible. In her midtwenties, Sarah was diagnosed with breast cancer, and she went down an unfamiliar path. The world didn't notice she went from a thriving student with a great future to a cancer patient on chemotherapy. They didn't see the trauma she endured of losing her hair and wondering if she was going to die.

But God met her in his love. God saw her when the world marched by. That love created a boldness in Sarah, a boldness that made her a person who sees the people the world doesn't notice and loves them in tangible ways.

Sarah continues her friendship with the girls she met on that train, and she even wrote a book about them called *The Invisible Girls*. Sarah could love Jesus in the faces of these Somalian girls because the Father had loved Sarah in the face of Jesus. It is this type of bold love that is pretty simple when we think about it. We just need to get off the train, go be with another, and discover Jesus in them.

The power of a story like Sarah's is that there is no hero, no parades being thrown in her honor. There is simply a person who was loved by Jesus and was set free to love others. That is true freedom. It is freedom because it's about Jesus, not about us. We love others by joining Jesus as he loves them. He loves them with the unending and unconditional love that he has been loved with by the Father for all eternity. When we begin to think that we can't love like that, we shouldn't worry. Jesus can. Find Jesus in the face of another person, and you will find a boldness to love that you didn't know you had.

You will be free to love boldly.

8

THE
BOLDNESS
OF
JUSTICE

It seems to me that love and hate, freedom and slavery, justice and injustice are never very far apart from each other. While I long for love, freedom, and justice, I have to admit that hate, slavery, and injustice are lurking inside of me as well. These conflicting realities can prevent us from moving forward. Too many people think that living a life of freedom means living a life free from the tensions that dwell in our hearts and in our world. The spiritual work that is set before us is finding and drinking in the love of the Father, Son, and Spirit in such a way that we realize there is room in that love for the hate in our hearts, the slavery in our addictions, and the injustices we commit. It is in us and in the world that God loves.

God's love has a much larger capacity than my own petty love, and it has room inside of it for much more complexity than most human love. It is not a love that requires the absence of hate, slavery, and injustice in order for it to be present. Rather, it is a love that wraps around those things and transforms them—softening them, breaking their outer shell, revealing something that lies dormant within them, and changing them into the fruit of the Spirit.

In order to be people of justice, we need to understand the spaciousness of God's love and Jesus's vision for what this love can look like when it shows up in the world.

Jesus's idea of living fully, loving boldly, and fearing nothing is extraordinary. The vision doesn't stop with us. It continues and spreads throughout the world so that the love of God shows up in God's people who work for his justice where they live. We are set free to be people who work for justice because the Trinity's love anchors our hearts. We are to work in the places where things are not the way they should be.

A Vision of Shalom

The Bible's vision of peace on earth is the vision of shalom. The word *shalom* is rich in meaning. In its basic sense, it is harmony between God and his people, God and his creation, and people and creation. Shalom is the way things are supposed to be. But shalom is not the way things are in our world.

Relationships are fractured between God and his people. Creation is groaning. Humans find ways to separate from one another rather than unite. Because of this relational fracturing, the world is a place of violence, vengeance, and volatility. Justice is needed, but it does not come cheap. Justice occurs when we work to bring the world back into God's vision of shalom. It won't happen all at once, and it is definitely work that goes against the tide of violence in the world and in our own hearts. But it is work that is possible because we have been set free by the love of God. That freedom changes how we see the world and how we see our neighbor.

If we are honest, the vision of shalom is overwhelming. What can we do in a world that has gone so sideways? Genocide, sex trafficking, racism, and war are just a few of the shalom-wrecking realities in the world that are too big for any of us to overcome by ourselves. I don't know about you, but when I get overwhelmed, it is easy for me to become passive. I can just sit back and watch the evening news, throw up my hands and pray, "Come, Lord Jesus," then raid the refrigerator before the football game starts.

What I don't want to admit in those moments is that the problem is not just out there among the worst offenders of injustice. The problem resides within me as well. Apathy, anger, violence, and discrimination exist within my own heart and every human heart. G. K. Chesterton is said to have been asked one time what the problem was with the world. His answer was simple and straightforward: "I am."

I am the problem. Until I recognize my own capacity to destroy shalom in the world, I will never work for justice. Worse than that, I may never seek the freedom that God offers me to bring his justice into the world through the radical revolution of his love.

Jesus knows how messed up the world is; he is not surprised or shocked by it. He knows how overwhelmed we get by the headlines and the evening news. He is also aware of our capacity for denial, which comes from our not seeing the injustice that resides in our own hearts. Which is why he calls us to a very simple and concrete vision of bringing shalom to bear on our world.

Jesus simply says, "Love your neighbor as yourself."

Simple enough. Yet despite how straightforward Jesus is, we find ways to take detours around that love. Rather than imagining ways we can love our neighbor, we sit back and get theological and philosophical about it. "Who's my neighbor? What's a neighbor? What's this 'neighbor' thing you speak of?" We are not much different from the people who originally heard those words. We are trying to avoid seeing and caring and serving our neighbor, the person nearest to us at any given moment. But if we have been set free by the love of the Father, Son, and Spirit, then we are free to be people who bring that love into our neighborhoods and work for justice.

I think the reason God created the world in a state of shalom is because shalom defines the relationships within the Trinity. The communion of Father, Son, and Spirit is a place of harmony and other-centeredness. There is no injustice in the Godhead, just the giving and receiving of divine love, which creates a context for unity, harmony, and peace. When we are called to be the people of this God who work for justice in the world, the call is not an empty command but a rich opportunity to show the love of God to the world around us in places where anti-shalom, if you will, has ruined people.

We also can catch a glimpse of the core problem with injustice in the world by looking at the shalom that exists within God. If shalom is the result of loving relationship, then injustice is the result of unloving relationship. While we need to work for political and policy solutions when it comes to the troubles of the world, they will never be quite enough. The problem of injustice is a relational one, not a political one.

When humanity divides itself into groups based on race, power, privilege, economics, social status, or geography, we create breeding grounds for injustice. We use our divisions to justify our separation from one another, and when we do that, we create the destructive powers of injustice. We can't see each other as image bearers of our Triune God because we have placed man-made labels over that image and allowed those labels to determine someone's worth or lack of worth.

A simple example of this is found in the immigration debate in America. I am not rendering a solution but making some observations. Think about the language we use for people who cross the border into our country to find work, albeit illegally. We call those people illegal aliens. Think about that! What comes to your mind? I think of slimy green monsters from outer space who have just broken out of jail, and no, I do not want those types of aliens in my country!

All over the world there are people who are deeply loved by the same Father who calls us a son or a daughter, people who are our brothers and sisters. What does it look like for us to take off the labels and see the image of God in them?

We don't simply use labels for those we see on the evening news, however. We use them for the people across the street, down the road, or across town. We label our neighbors who are gay, Muslim, or divorced. We label the neighborhood a few blocks away from us with all the Russian immigrants.

We don't see people who are made in the image of the God who sets us free to love them, because we separate ourselves from them through our differences. When we do that, we take away their light as image bearers of God and create separation that robs us of the possibility of knowing them.

That is why Jesus confronts injustice not by calling our attention to the greatest offenders of shalom but by calling us to love our neighbor as ourselves. We like the idea that we are made in the image of God, but do we like the idea that our neighbors are too?

When Jesus tells us to "love your neighbor as yourself," he places justice within our reach through the proactive power of neighborliness. Despite the fact that in our broken world there are many systemic and global issues we should be aware of and fight for, there are issues going on right around us in the place where we've been called to live and do life. The call to love our neighbor is a call for us to get involved and work with Jesus to create a just world.

Jesus knows we can't truly understand all the problems of the world without becoming paralyzed by their weight. But we don't need to carry the weight. That's why Jesus brings justice. However, we are to be the kingdom of God on earth, and we can bring justice in small ways. This is why the call to love our neighbor is so powerful.

So what will it take for us to work for justice? It is a simple first step of walking across the street. We need to take the powerful freedom we have experienced through the love of the Father and extend it to another who has been equally made in his image and is equally loved.

A Battle

As we reach out to another, we'll find justice, but we'll also be met with internal tension and sometimes with internal confrontation. When I extend grace to another, I am often confronted with the injustice in my own heart. I have to fight the labels I have placed on people around me, the judgments I have made, and the walls of separation I am so comfortable hiding behind. I am confronted by the fact that while I find Jesus's vision of loving my neighbor to be a good thing, something else often consumes my energy: my own self-interest.

Sadly, I am comfortable with the separation I cause, which also means I am comfortable with a certain amount of injustice. Because of this, I can't love my neighbor. In our separation, I can't see my neighbor. I'm too busy worrying about what's mine. One of the best examples of this is when I go to a play or a movie that is really crowded. When I finally make it past all the people and walk through the door of the theater, what's the first thing I do? I say, "I've got to save seats." It's funny to watch people like me lay our coats and jackets and purses out over the seats as if we are staking a claim on a piece of land. These are my seats! The greatest act of injustice occurs when someone dares to try taking my seats!

In order for me to overcome my individualism, I have to first recognize and confess my own propensity for greed and self-interest. We have to confess that this attitude in us is the same attitude of those who trample over people on Black Friday to get the greatest deal on a game console for their kids, or those who sit by comfortably in our rampant consumer economy while thousands of people around the world go without clean water. It's not that we don't care or don't think those things are tragic; it's just that when we are busy trying to get what's ours and keep other people from taking it, we don't have much energy for caring about another person. Our individualism creates the very real possibility that our neighborhoods are going to hell, quite literally. But we find it hard to care about the fact that there is injustice going on in the world around us because we are filled with our own entitlement.

The Freedom to Love Our Neighbor

But that is no longer our story. We have been given the radical gift of grace. The good God who loves us as Father, Son, and Spirit has set us free from self-interest. God's love deconstructs our individualism and claims.

In the economy of shalom, God's love sets us free to see his image in our neighbor. The recognition that our value and worth come from that image unites us all despite our differences, and it empowers us to celebrate those differences because they point us back to the love of the Father. Grace teaches us that all is given and nothing is earned, which frees us to love and to seek justice.

This type of freedom allows us to join God's revolution of resurrecting the neighborhood. We don't have to live in fear of losing what's ours, because we have been set free by the one who moved into the neighborhood to take on our flesh, to live our life, and to die our death. He invites us to participate with him as he brings his shalom to the world. In Jesus, the Father declared that nothing is earned and all is given. And there's enough to go around.

We are free because we're no longer asking what's ours. We're asking what's best, what's true, what's right. The kind of grace we're talking about creates energy that we can invest in our neighborhoods to make them places of justice.

What does this look like?

If nothing is earned and all is given, then we realize that Jesus has given us everything. He has given us resources to invest in our neighborhoods: gifts, talents, passions, interests, eyes to see, hearts to care, hands to serve. And he's given all of that so we can create new possibilities for the other—the person we've walked by, the person we've ignored, the disabled person in the wheelchair, the homeless man, the single mom across the street, the family who just moved here from Somalia, the person who is not like us but is living in close proximity to us.

What would it mean for us to identify local injustices and inequities and to cry out? We are empowered by the command to love our neighbor as ourselves, to realize that we belong to the communities around us. We can't passively drive by and be glad we don't live there. What if we allowed the peace of God in our hearts to move us to roll up our sleeves and work for justice?

The dream of the neighborhood is dependent upon courageous neighbors who will restructure their lives, reorganize their priorities, and realign their values to bring about the possibility of shalom—the harmony between us and God, us and creation, us and our neighbor. We need to move past fear. We need to take a look at our lives and not just be content that we wrote a check.

It's going to take a little bit more.

As you dream about how you're going to reorganize your life to work for shalom, consider your gifts. Perhaps you can start a small business that empowers underprivileged workers, or a coffee shop that is run by people with disabilities, or a booth at the local market on Saturday where refugees can sell their cultural crafts.

I know some doctors and nurses who scaled back on living expenses so that they can work less and offer free medical care. It wasn't easy. They had to research and figure out issues with insurance, writing prescriptions, and legal liability. But they did it! They moved past the fear, hassle, and legality and were free to love.

One woman who is an art educator in an environment where all the art funding is being cut brings shalom to her neighborhood by creating art programs for elementary and junior high students. The impact is enormous in the lives of these kids and their families.

A man who is an incredible handyman fixes neighbors' houses for free. He has been infused with grace. He goes into a world of people who can't afford to fix their roof or window or porch, and he creates shalom. He's resurrecting the neighborhood.

There is beauty in this shalom. And in this grace not only are we given energy to get to work but also energy to dance, to celebrate, and to throw great parties. We find energy to dance in the midst of the neighborhood because Jesus is resurrected from the dead, because justice is rolling in, and because we get to participate in announcing that there's another world, and it's breaking in with us.

Justice starts with a dream. It starts with energy that comes from grace. It starts because we have been set free from self-centeredness and are free to love another.

Justice, in its purest form, can be expressed in the simple, profound call to neighborliness. What does it mean for us to love our neighbor? There's geography, there's nearness, there's a relationship, and to act neighborly is a simple, profound revolution. Neighborliness requires that we enter into our neighbor's story with the love of God and that we genuinely care about their story's outcome.

In loving our neighbor, we take responsibility for the environment in which our children are raised, our elderly die, and our disabled are cared for. You can tell a lot about a neighborhood by what they do with their dying. What do they do with newborns? What do they do with those who can't produce or perform and there's no room for them in the rat race of the consumer-driven, you-get-ahead-by-what-you-earn mentality?

There's always a place at the table in a world where nothing is earned and all is given.

Justice comes when all sectors of culture are filled with people who see a world that is not yet here and are working to clear a path for its coming. How do we create livable-wage jobs for people who need a second chance? How do we restructure, reorganize, and realign our values to love our neighbor? How do we do this as educators? How do we do this as businesspeople? How do we inspire people to see this issue of injustice differently? How do we dream about what it means to create Jesus's justice in the neighborhood of government, of law, of family—where all sectors of culture are invested with people who have both the freedom and the grace to infuse and invest and create new possibilities?

The dream of the neighborhood is nothing shy of a micro-revolution in which ordinary people like you and me overcome apathy and self-interest through courageous acts of self-giving and love, and it can only happen because Jesus sets us free to do it. I've seen it.

I've watched as churches have rallied to Jesus's vision of the neighborhood too. I've seen thousands of people show up to serve local public schools. I've talked to city commissioners who said there's no other group of people they can call who will show up and follow through. One school district had all the funds to continue its school lunch program in the summer, and they had places to do it, but they didn't have volunteers. The commissioner made one phone call to one pastor, who rallied the other pastors, and we staffed the lunch program for the entire summer for the entire city.

I don't say this to promote anyone in particular. We are people who spent the majority of our lives saving our seats. We're not good people; we're not the heroes of the story. We're bad people who, given the right conditions, would steal those kids' lunches. But we're people who are following the dusty footprints of a rabbi who moved into our neighborhood and resurrected it. We're people who are living into a dream of what it means to die to self and live to God. We're people who have the energy because we've been infused with grace. We're people who get to proclaim to the world with our voices and our lives that our King is raised, and that changes everything.

Justice is a dream that is realized one ordinary person at a time, one neighborhood at a time. This is a dream you're called to participate in with your ordinary life, infused with the freedom of Jesus's love. This is a dream that starts a revolution that doesn't stop. It's the revolution in which we love our neighbor as ourselves, and that will change the world.

9

FEAR NOTHING

It's easy to talk about living a life without fear when things are going well. We know those moments when life runs with ease. Our family is healthy, we get a raise at our job, and our relationships are strong and growing.

But what do we do when life doesn't deal us a good hand? How do we live in freedom when the doctor says the word *cancer*, when our kids are hurting, or when we get laid off? What do we do when God, in all his goodness, seems hidden and the only things visible are the difficulties and uncertainties we face? Do we run away from God and hide? Do we crash into depression? Do we lose hope? I do all of those things in the face of fear.

Fear is powerful because it threatens us with the absence of love and life. If "the one" rejects us, will we be alone forever? If the cancer has its way, how many months will we have left? If our kids hurt, where will the resources come from to help them? If we lose our job, will we find a new job so that we can make ends meet?

What we long for in these moments is security. Who—or what—can offer us security in the midst of life's greatest fears?

Fear shows up in these times with faith-crushing power and threatens to separate us from all that we love. It drives a wedge between God and us and asks, "Can you trust God now?"

God has the power to create security in our hearts when we face life's greatest challenges. His love brings us freedom from our fear. That doesn't mean there is no pain or loss or suffering. We are guaranteed we will experience hurt and unexpected life events that discourage us. But God's love is larger than the fears we face when things are uncertain. This is a love that promises to meet us in the midst of our panicked moments, and it's a love that carries us through them to the end. When we breathe our last breath and fear smiles as if it has won, God's love is there. And it's greater than any fear.

The love of the Father, Son, and Spirit frees us to live fully and love boldly but also to face our fears. The love of God is the security we long for and are invited to cling to in the moments when life seems to deal us a crushing blow and everything seems uncertain.

Uncertainty is the place where our good and loving God meets us in our fear and asks us to stand firm. Some of our deepest cries for freedom come from the places of our deepest fears. We want to be free from a world of loss and suffering. Our pleas are authentic.

There are two things that can bring us freedom in the midst of fear: perfect love and the Holy Spirit.

First John 4:18 tells us, "There is no fear in love. But perfect love drives out fear, because fear has to do with punishment. The one who fears is not made perfect in love."

The love of the Father, Son, and Spirit is perfect love. It is a love that is unconditional. It is a love that is not based on performance, because there is nothing we can do to earn it. It is a love that has existed in perfection before time. The Father loves the Son perfectly, the Son loves the Father perfectly, and the Spirit expresses this love perfectly. We were given access to this love when God sent his Son to die on the cross and when the Son left his Spirit to intercede for us and to cry out for us when we're so far in despair that we don't even have words to speak.

When this perfect love encounters fear, John tells us that it powerfully confronts it. It drives out fear because fear is associated with punishment. When we hit the rough patches in life, one of the first thoughts we have is that God is mad at us. Have you ever thought that?

When we face pain or loss or when we suffer, such times can challenge our faith. We live in a culture that thrives on instant gratification, pleasure, and pain avoidance. We're conditioned to think that if we live good lives nothing bad should happen to us. The lies of cultural prosperity have blinded us to some basic realities of life. Jesus said it this way in John 16:33: "I have told you these things, so that in me you may have peace. In this world you will have trouble. But take heart! I have overcome the world."

When we are set free to see the world for what it is, a broken place with both beauty and suffering, we are also set free from the false assumption that we will never experience pain. In fact, we are set free to face suffering . . . with courage.

Persevering in Fear

The fear that slaps us around in our suffering doesn't magically leave us overnight. It rears its head even as we fight it, but it loses its footing as perfect love drives it out.

When I was younger, I was a lineman on my football team. It was pretty much the only position for someone of my size and speed. Being five foot ten and 275 pounds didn't scream, "Give me the ball!" to my coaches. Despite my dreams of running the ball, I was clearly suited for standing in front of another guy and pushing him out of the way (and oftentimes being pushed!).

One of the main jobs of a lineman is to drive the player in front of him off the ball so that the running back has room to make the play and gain yards. To prepare for this, in practice we would push around a giant blocking sled. It was a massive metal monster. It had six sections on it so that six guys could push it around the practice field. It was a sight to see! The coach would stand on the sled, adding 300 pounds of his own weight, and scream at us, "Drive, drive, drive!" When game time came, all the hours of pushing the sled around prepared us to drive our opponents backward so that our team could move the ball down the field and eventually score. If we were lucky, we'd win.

This football scenario is what I see when I hear the words "perfect love drives out fear" from the passage in 1 John. This passage doesn't suggest that there isn't resistance or that the work happens without pain and sweat and faith. Driving out fear is hard work, but it's love's work, not ours.

Love confronts fear and pushes it back. We are loved with the Father's love and brought into this family of perfect love for no other reason than that the God who is Father, Son, and Spirit loves us for who we are.

The Holy Spirit has been given to us as a seal securing our place at God's table. He is active in pouring the love of God into our hearts and comforting us in the midst of our suffering. The Holy Spirit is the tangible presence of love that gives us the power to stand our ground in the face of fear, while he drives out that fear with his perfect love. Perfect love drives fear back and gives us the freedom to face it and to trust that we're loved unconditionally and eternally.

I have seen others sit in the most tragic moments and yet stand strong in their faith. They showed me that they can truly sense the love of God residing in the place of fear. I have watched that perfect love hold families together as their young child goes through six months of life-threatening chemotherapy. I've seen it comfort a close friend who received a phone call that her husband died on the way to work. I've seen it strengthen people who went from being healthy and vibrant to bound by a debilitating disease and living the rest of their life in a wheelchair. Each one will tell you that because of God's perfect love, they were not afraid. They believed in and experienced God's love in the midst of their greatest fear. They were secure in that love because of the Holy Spirit.

A Different Story?

There are moments when I don't feel like the Holy Spirit is doing all of that. There are moments when it seems as though my faith does not amount to much. If I am honest,

I let fear into those places. Sometimes it looks like anxiety. Other times the fear goes deep within my spirit, leaving me feeling numb.

Times like this have been referred to as "dark nights of the soul" by some of the early church's mystics, like St. John of the Cross. These dark nights are times when it seems as if God removes his presence from us. These are desert times.

When I think of my daughter, Kaylee, and try to imagine her future, I experience a wide range of emotions, including fear. Having a mental disability leaves her vulnerable, and one day her mom and I won't be around to take care of her. What happens then?

Fear sits just below the surface in these seasons, even though I see God at work all around me, even though I see him perform miracles in my life and in others' lives. But that miracle hasn't come for Kaylee. There has been no sudden healing or even an opportunity for such healing. Where is God in the middle of that fear, the kind that shakes your heart?

You might have something like this going on in your life too. Maybe there is something you can't seem to figure out, and nothing makes sense. Maybe you're experiencing loss or grief or suffering. Whatever it is, you just know deep within you that this is not the way life was supposed to be.

I wish I could tell you, "Perfect love casts out fear! It all gets better!" But I would be lying. Instead, I tell you this: walking with my daughter for the last twenty-one years has opened up a space in me. A desert space. A dark night of the soul. My desert space is not completely dark. It's like dusk. I sit in that place. There are no questions anymore. I have asked them all. But something happens in that space. I learn about myself and God and life and Kaylee.

This is a desert place where all my previous encounters with the presence of God seem to have vacated the premises. At times, I wonder if God has abandoned me here. Or if God has abandoned Kaylee. I don't think he has, but sometimes I wonder. For the longest time, I ran from it. It's scary. It's quiet. But as time has passed and I've learned more about God and his perfect love, I've stopped trying to escape it. I don't try to change it. Instead, it's a place where fear has been driven out *and yet* suffering still remains.

This is a place I am growing to appreciate. It is teaching me about my own need to control and to fix and to make the world the way I want it. It has shown me that I spend more time protesting God than trusting him. It has shown me that I haven't believed that I am loved in all the ways I have described in this book. So I sit here and learn (and relearn) about the love that God has for me and my daughter.

This is an honest place, and in a real sense, this is freedom. Not the visions of freedom I made up in my own mind but a real freedom. It is a freedom from fear and self and all the fears that the self carries around inside.

There is a duality. This is a difficult place . . . but it's also a safe place.

This is what leads me to believe that we don't have to fear these places. Perhaps the desert place is not a desert place at all but a place where God is meeting me in his love. It just doesn't come to me the way I pictured it. Maybe the desert is God and the silence is love and the end result will be the freedom to trust.

10

COMPELLED BY LOVE

There is a picture of the church inside my head. I know there is nothing super exciting about the church for most people. I didn't grow up in the church, so I don't have a lot of baggage about the whole thing. Don't get me wrong. I have seen my fair share of goofiness and stupidity. I hate the tabloid version of the church that is portrayed on the internet or in the media, but I hate even more that we oftentimes earn that reputation by being goofy and stupid.

I can't shake the picture in my head though. It is a vision that is informed by the Bible, not by the goofiness, and it's a beautiful one. It's a vision of this amazing garden that is full of every kind of plant and fruit, flower and vegetable. Beauty surrounds it, but it's not pristine; it's organic, messy even, but still profoundly beautiful. There is always something in season, some good and gracious harvest that is ready for the taking. And people come from all over to pick its flowers and fruit. It is there, in the middle of the city, sustaining, beautifying, and offering itself to all who desire it.

It is, I believe, our true vocation to offer the life of Jesus to the world through our own self-giving. My vision is not stupid or goofy but compelling to me, deep in my soul.

I have been pastoring the church Imago Dei Community for thirteen years. What began in a living room God moved to the middle of a city. We continue to ask him what he is inviting us to be as a part of his kingdom on earth. In asking this question, I discovered the heart that Jesus is looking for by reading about the life of Paul in 2 Corinthians 5.

One of the things I love about the apostle Paul is that when he spoke about Christ, he *persuaded* people. He didn't show up and condemn them. He didn't rule them with laws and codes. He persuaded them.

Paul was able to persuade people to believe that Jesus was the Savior of the world in part because he lived a persuasive life. Before he was set free by the love of God, Paul persecuted those who followed Christ. He wanted to see Christians die. He lived a life of hatred, anger, and violence.

But then Paul had a radical encounter with Jesus. Paul was so completely changed that when he spoke with people about Jesus, they could look at his life and see how Jesus had changed him. Jesus took him from being a man of self-righteous violence to being a lover of God and others. That is a persuasive life.

Paul makes me think of the lives of those who believe in God today. I stop and ask myself, "Are we persuasive people?" Are people becoming curious about Jesus because of the lives we're living together in community? The hard truth is . . . probably not. An unpersuasive life is not good news for the world. If our lives don't exude the aroma of freedom in Christ, our faith will not compel people to be attracted to the God we claim to know and worship.

In all honesty, I think the image I had of God in the past was of a God I didn't even like, let alone love. The false image of an Almighty being consumed by his own self-interest is not the loving and good God who is Father, Son, and Spirit. If I was not persuaded to love the God I say I believe in, why would anyone else be?

There is a huge difference between religious duty and relational desire. Our God is beautiful and attractive. I want to move toward him because I see a relationship within him of love and goodness. I want to be a part of that.

When we find ourselves serving or worshiping or even telling people about a god who is not the beautiful God of the Trinity, we are serving a god we don't really like. Maybe we have a sense of obligation to a higher power, but that's birthed out of religious duty or guilt, not love. And duty and guilt are never compelling. To the outside world, our religion appears to be confining and claustrophobic, anything but free.

The love that compelled Paul came from a very different God—the God we have been learning about in these chapters. The Father, Son, and Spirit. This God was so fundamentally different from the gods of Paul's day because God exuded grace, mercy, love, and hope. And everyone could experience his love through faith. Paul responded to God's love by surrendering to him, and that love also moved him to persuade others that God loved them too. He wanted people to know

Jesus, and he was willing to lay aside everything, including his life and comfort and security, to tell anyone who would listen.

Compelled by Guilt or by Love?

What compels you?

One of the things I'm thrilled about in our Imago Dei Community is that over the years our city has seen persuasiveness. The churches of Portland are together loving, serving, and blessing the city. Conversations are taking place in the streets and in city hall about why we in the church would love and serve and give ourselves away. We are living persuasive lives.

When Paul writes to the church in Corinth, there are all sorts of issues in the church. There are issues in their relationships with Paul, with God, and with each other. Paul says this:

> Since, then, we know what it is to fear the Lord, we try to persuade others. What we are is plain to God, and I hope it is also plain to your conscience. We are not trying to commend ourselves to you again, but are giving you an opportunity to take pride in us, so that you can answer those who take pride in what is seen rather than in what is in the heart. If we are "out of our mind," as some say, it is for God; if we are in our right mind, it is for you. For Christ's love compels us, because we are convinced that one died for all, and therefore all died. And he died for all, that those who live should no longer live for themselves but for him who died for them and was raised again. (2 Cor. 5:11–15)

Living a persuasive life shows up when people who claim to know Jesus are compelled by love for Jesus and his love for other people. Most Christians I talk to are compelled by guilt, not by love. And I think we're compelled by guilt because we don't believe in the love of Christ.

Have you ever had somebody do something for you and then you felt obligated to repay them? It feels like they were just waiting for you to have a need so they could throw it in your face, and now you owe them. Maybe a parent loaned you money, and you have to hear about it every year. Or a neighbor helped you fix your sprinklers, and now you have to go to all of their parties. For most of us, if we could go back in time and never have needed that person, we would feel free. We would be free from obligation. We would be free from the weight of guilt.

Being compelled by guilt does not make for a persuasive life. Nobody out there is saying, "I wish I had what you have because you seem miserable and guilt-ridden." Or, "I wish I knew what you know about God so I could feel like he is disappointed in me too! That looks fun!" If we are persuaded by guilt to serve Jesus, there's a pretty good chance we won't be persuading anyone else. We and others can be compelled by love only if we have the good God of Scripture as our starting point.

Paul understood this. He understood the God of Scripture. Father, Son, and Spirit live together in a perfect communion of love. The Father always loves the Son; the Son always loves the Father; the Spirit mediates this love between them. They don't need anything outside of themselves to complete them. They are a community of perfection within themselves. They didn't *need* worshipers. They didn't ask, "How will I get love? I'd better create someone to love me," because they already had love.

There is no obligation. The Father, Son, and Spirit did not choose to love us so we could feel guilty. *They love us because they just do.* They didn't need us. They wanted us.

Creation was not a divine scheme to get people to need God. So what was God's motive in creating us? Creation was an overflow and an extension of his love. This good Father, good Son, and good Spirit who live in this good communion of love wanted to bring others into their love.

We know how the story goes, right? The fall happened after creation. In our freedom, we didn't choose this love and inclusion and communion. Instead, we chose independence and autonomy and rebellion. We fractured our relationship with God. Even so, we didn't catch God off guard. God never said, "Oh my! What will I do? What happened? How can I guilt them back into worshiping me?"

He wanted to redeem us, to turn sinful rebels back into sons and daughters so that we could be included in this love, this communion of Father, Son, and Holy Spirit. Paul describes it this way in 2 Corinthians 5:14–15:

> For Christ's love compels us, because we are convinced that one died for all, and therefore all died. And he died for all, that those who live should no longer live for themselves but for him who died for them and was raised again.

Jesus paid for our sin so that he could turn us back to the Father. He didn't die for us and rescue us from our sin because he *had* to or because he *needed* more worshipers. He did it because he wanted to and because he loves us.

The God who exists in a perfect communion of love is more loving than we believe he is. If we could get a glimpse of all that God is as Father, Son, and Spirit, we would be compelled to respond. Compelled by love, not by guilt.

People who live persuasive lives through which others are attracted to, interested in, and want to talk about Jesus are people who are compelled by love. They know they are free to love others because Christ loves them and others. This knowledge reorders their lives and their world.

Are you compelled by love, or are you compelled by guilt? Jesus sets you free to be loved by the Father through the Son in the Spirit.

Re-created

When we're compelled by love, there's even more freedom to be found. People who live persuasive lives experience new creation. New creation is the reality that through Jesus Christ's life, death, and resurrection, we are brought into the love of the Father through the Son by the Spirit because we are united with Jesus and made completely new creations in him.

Paul continues:

> So from now on we regard no one from a worldly point of view. Though we once regarded Christ in this way, we do so no longer. Therefore, if anyone is in Christ, the new creation has come: The old has gone, the new is here! (2 Cor. 5:16–17)

When I became a follower of Jesus, I was eighteen years old. The next day someone could have looked at my life and said that nothing had really changed. From the outside looking in, it probably just looked like I had started going to church. But from my personal, internal world and from Jesus's point of view, everything had changed. Before Christ entered my life, I was an enemy of God. I was someone who didn't think about God, who ignored God, who didn't care about God. I was someone who had his back turned to God. Only through the love of Christ did God turn me back to himself.

Inside me there was peace and harmony, and there hasn't been a day since when I haven't thought about God. The new creation I experienced, that moment I met Christ, has been with me and growing and expanding in my life ever since.

Paul tells us that something happens when we experience new creation. We no longer think of God in the court of public opinion. We actually know him as the God to whom the world belongs. We know him as the one who is bringing a new creation that is breaking in to this world, and we know him as the one who creates us in a new way. We know him as our hope and the world's hope. We see that God is not a God of abandonment but a God who is present and active in our lives and in the world. He is a God who declared through his own death and resurrection that our past does not have the final word. Our future exists within his new creation.

For some of you, it's hard to let your heart believe that. But the promise and hope of the gospel is that our past is not going to dictate our future. We may be experiencing a slow process of change, but the new creation is breaking in. It is here and it is coming, and it promises that there will clearly be a day when we are completely without sin before the face of Jesus. People who believe in that are hopeful people. Hopeful people are persuasive people.

A signpost of new creation is freedom. New creation promises freedom in our lives where in the past, perhaps, there was entanglement. We think of all the places where we aren't free. We might not feel free in our attraction to money or to people. We don't feel free from our addictions or habits or past or anxieties. However, the hope of new creation is that it's anchored in the person of Jesus. "It is for freedom that Christ has set us free" (Gal. 5:1).

The kind of love that compels us is a love that sets us free. That's new creation. I wasn't free, and now Christ has released me. I'm free. You're free. We're compelled by love to have hope and experience freedom.

We can begin to dream new dreams because the love of God has made us new. We have a new hope and a new freedom from guilt and shame. There is freedom when we're sons and daughters of God. This freedom invites us into a courageous life.

I believe that if we can replace the false image of God that produces guilt in us with the biblical image of the good God who is Father, Son, and Spirit, we will become persuasive people without thinking about it. When we find within us the Spirit's desire to love the Father and the Son and to love those around us, new creation dreams begin to rise up inside of us. We are compelled by love.

The Final Cry

We are a people who cried out for freedom. This cry led us down dark paths only to find slavery waiting for us at the end. I hope you can see that God heard our cries and that he never quit listening. I hope you can see that he answered our cries by setting us free in his love. I hope you can see how beautiful and good God really is.

The world is crying out for freedom too. It's crying out for the love of the God who set us free. I am hopeful because I know that when we are set free to love God, it's only a matter of time before we join him in answering the cries we hear around us in the hearts of others.

When God's people are set free in his love and compelled to love others, a beautiful announcement that the Father, Son, and Spirit have come to bring home all who are lost will fall from our lips and our lives. When that happens, we will be persuasive people who show others the love of the Father, Son, and Spirit.

The lost will return home, where they will find freedom and love.

11

THE
JOURNEY
AHEAD

I wish that everything I have ever preached or written or learned I had also experienced. But the truth is that there are many things I am still living into. I suppose it will be that way for the rest of my life.

This book has been an invitation to a journey into freedom that has been made available to us through the love of the Father in the gift of the Son through the power of the Spirit. It is an invitation I pray we will take seriously, for I believe that if we do, we will find ourselves becoming who we were truly created to be: people who live fully, love boldly, and fear nothing.

It is important, though, before we end that I warn you that this journey into freedom is not an easy one. It requires us to fight the fight of faith, to stand firmly rooted in the truth that the God we claim to believe in is in fact the God who is Father, Son, and Spirit and that we have been included in the love between them.

That is no easy task in a world full of pain and loss and suffering. Perhaps even more of a threat is that this spiritual journey has to compete with sales pitches for an easier way, a nonrelational, self-help, pick-yourself-up-by-the-bootstraps sort of way. The way of Jesus to the Father by the Spirit is often threatened by the contemporary spiritualities of our day.

The Insufficiency of Contemporary Spiritualities

I am suspicious of contemporary spiritualities that reduce life to cheap taxonomies, selling us on self-improvement methods that will help us achieve the life we always wanted but can somehow never attain. These spiritualities are insufficient for the complexity of the life we are called to live, and they are disrespectful of that complexity. The issues of pain, sin, tragedy, and death have no place in the simplified spiritual remedies, which offer false hope in the face of the realities of living.

Such spiritualities are insufficient because they are not soul forming. They may offer counsel for moments when we want an immediate how-to that will allow us to escape our uncomfortable situation, but they in fact help us to avoid the soul in order to change the situation. What is needed is a transformation that goes beyond the circumstance and subverts the very temptation to escape or control these moments. Avoiding them through cheap spiritual remedies only steals the soul-forming context in which the Holy Spirit does his finest work.

These spiritualities are also insufficient because they are dishonest. They offer us a life that would never even be aspired to by most of the world. They are spiritual products produced in a culture of mass affluence that is inappropriate to the work of true gospel formation. Gospel formation by its very nature is acultural. It is a timeless work that offers healing and salvation to the people in Darfur as well as in Dallas.

Any spirituality that requires an individual to live in a context of political freedom and economic abundance in order to work is not a spirituality that is centered in the gospel. Gospel spirituality is soul forming for those who live in great suffering as well as for those who live in great abundance. It is the same spiritual journey for both souls. Yet, it is attended to in different ways.

If our spiritual lives are not being shaped by the Father, Son, and Spirit, whose love comes to us in the same way regardless of race, culture, or economics, then we need to be suspicious of such spiritualities.

I have a hunch that what happens to many Christians in the context of affluence is that the love of God is missed. Spirituality is reduced to superstition, not in a mythological sense but in a consumer sense. We barter with God in order to get what we want from him. We give our money, pray our prayers, and read our Bible with unspoken, hidden motives, believing that if we place the appropriate action in the heavenly coin slot we will get the outcome we desire. Our marriage will work, we will find the spouse of our dreams, our kids will turn out right, and we will have safe travels on our road trip.

It is an odd economic relationship we have with God because our appeasing of him never seems to end in the quantified results we desire. When we reduce spiritual practices to this sort of give-and-take trade-off, then we have in fact changed the core nature of gospel spirituality to a consumer superstition through which we hope to keep the God of power and sovereignty on our good side. Relationship is missed, the soul is bypassed, and the raw material of pain, sin, doubt, need, and suffering is ignored rather than offered to the God who redeems these things and reshapes the landscape of our inner lives through Jesus.

If we want to live in the freedom that is offered to us in the love of God, we must stand guard against these spiritual remedies that lead to death, not life.

The Truth of Scripture

Living into the love of God is a life journey. This means it may take decades and generations. The life we hope for may be lived by our grandchildren rather than by us. Our lives are not going to change in ninety days. Soul formation is process oriented, not production driven.

This book is an invitation into relationship. Relationships bring us intimacy and belonging, significance and communion. They are not simply products we use to make us who we want to be. With that approach, the relationship is breached and someone is used. The Father, Son, and Spirit love us and offer us the freedom to be not our own little gods but his beloved sons and daughters who experience what it means to be fully alive and fully free.

The greatest safeguard in all of this for me has been listening to Scripture and seeing the honesty and rawness with which God has allowed himself to be revealed. If we want to live in the freedom we have been given in the love of God, then we need to allow Scripture to shape our souls and protect us from spiritual lies.

Sacred Scripture is losing popularity in this climate of consumer spiritualities. The arguments over inerrancy and infallibility have given way to an attitude of dismissal by some. The dissection of the biblical narrative into propositions that are removed from context has been used to sell God to an entire generation of people who are not overly interested in him.

I was given my first Bible when I was eighteen. It was a hardcover book that had far more pages than anything I had ever attempted to read. I was grateful for it; I still own it.

As I cracked it open, I was shocked by what I read. The stories were raw and seemingly unedited of people's sins and failures, doubts and troubles. I was glad I wasn't one of the characters in the Bible because I didn't want to have my life story told that honestly. But I also saw that the Bible is filled with the story of redemption by a great God who came into all that rawness and sin with a salvation that was more raw, brutal, and wonderful than anything I had ever read about.

I was surprised how poorly the lives of people in Scripture were modeled for me in the faith community I was part of at that time. The people who came to hear this book preached to them on Sunday morning appeared to have just had a makeover. They didn't have a hangover like Noah did when he finally reached land. They didn't seem to be in relationships of violent conflict like Cain and Abel. They didn't cry out with weeping like the psalmist did. The book I had in my hands was a dangerous book for people whose lives were on the brink of disaster and who were in need of a supernatural salvation. The people I sat among didn't seem to have any of these problems.

If you read the Bible at face value, you would think that the people who hold this book as their revelation for faith and life would show up dressed in protective helmets and shoulder pads, like football players ready for a game of life that is going to kick the crap out of them. God is alive, redeeming, interceding, listening, judging, delivering, saving, and shaking humanity to its core.

Nothing I have ever read has dealt with the issues of life and relationships and faith so honestly. It was the way in which the truth was revealed in this holy book that sucked me into a life of faith by the Holy Spirit.

I often think we would have a better picture of our spiritual reality if we just rolled out of bed and came to church in our pajamas. Messy hair, bad breath, unkempt faces, and wrinkled clothes—the raw humility of our humanity. Nothing about us would be prideful. Nothing *could* be prideful. We would be there together in our fragile state as people who need to sleep several hours a night just to get through another day.

I don't think that will ever happen, but Scripture is that honest. It speaks to our situation with a brutal honesty that most of us have been taught to hide from. Yet, it is here in our actual state of need that God performs his soul-shaping work of redemption through the gospel of Jesus.

I fear that we have lost our appetite for truth. The Bible is not a book to be dissected and studied in the confines of a sterile laboratory faith. It is a book written to meet life on the bare pavement. God is at work in the long story of redemption, and he, being the truth, is truthful in the way he tells the story.

In this sacred book of honest revelation, there is a loving Father behind the revelation who initiates his soul-forming work in Jesus through the power of the Holy Sprit. The work of spiritual formation is primarily God's work that we receive and in which we participate. We don't create it, capture it, or consume it. We are included in it by his grace. We live with God by grace, and in the living we are changed. God's soul-forming work of his Spirit shapes us into the image of Jesus over the course of a lifetime. In our formation, we begin living kingdom lives as we participate in life given and received in grace.

The world in which we are attempting to live out our belonging to the Father, Son, and Spirit is a world that continues to try to deceive us into taking a shortcut to a quicker fix. The reason I love Scripture is because it anchors my heart in the truth that there are no shortcuts. There is only relationship. The words of God protect me from thinking that somehow the story can be reduced and sold.

We get to keep ourselves storied in the love story. A Father seeks a bride for his Son and prepares her by the Holy Spirit. And despite our feeble attempts at holiness, despite our outright rebellion, he keeps coming after us with salvation, redemption, and relationship.

When we choose slavery, he brings freedom.

When we choose isolation, he brings us into relationship.

When we choose sin, he brings forgiveness.

And the story never ends, because the love of the Father, Son, and Spirit is inexhaustible.

The Power of Imagination

So perhaps we can end by simply using our imagination. What does it look like for us to step into the freedom of the love of God? What could it look like for us to be caught up in the mystery of this love?

Caught up into this mystery, I can't help but lean heavily on my imagination. The magnitude of the love of the Father, Son, and Spirit requires me to tap into my imagination because this love and goodness is otherworldly. The story captures my imagination and calls me into the depths of worshipful devotion. The in-breaking reign of love within me, through me, and about me calls forth something deep that only a God-directed imagination can behold.

But then subtle unbelief creeps in, inviting me to live a reduced life outside the story of royal love and divine goodness. The ordinariness of needing to take a shower, brush my teeth, eat breakfast, and let the dog out beckons me into a loveless stupor. Amid the daily duties of taking the kids to school, picking up the groceries, and going to work, I find this miracle story pushed to the side. I am given to the ordinary, and my eyes are covered by the veil of evening news and reality TV.

Nothing in this ordinariness changes the miraculous reality of God's love. I have simply neglected to see that within this ordinariness I have allowed imagination to fail or fall away.

So what do I do?

I do not play make-believe like a child. Nowhere am I required to make anything up. I am required to pay attention in a new way, to see not through the lens of fairy tale and make-believe but through the lens of redeemed imagination—imagination only necessary here and now in this temporary veil of material life. I imagine the possibility of God's love breaking into my world in my heart and through my life. In imagining, I am called into a love that makes me wholly alive.

Without this imagination, faith has nowhere to lay its head. I am reduced to tasks and duty. Desire is discarded. But here within the framework of a heart captured by the love of God, I see a world of possibility, a world in which the reign of love is everywhere breaking in and the noise of futility fades. Here I see with the eyes of faith that I am the beloved and he is mine. I see that I have been set free and brought into the Father's house of love. I taste the Spirit's cry within my heart that God is my Abba Father. And there in that moment, I am fully alive with a bold love, nothing to fear, and a Father who embraces me in the face of Jesus through the presence of the Holy Spirit. I am home.

ACKNOWLEDGMENTS

I am grateful for all who worked with me to bring this book into being. I am forever indebted to my friend and mentor Ron Frost, who first started me down the path of trinitarian theology. It has been a great blessing and something God has used to help me see how truly good and beautiful he is. Also, Michael Reeves's book *Delighting in the Trinity* was instrumental for me in this season. It is well worth your time to read to see how the rich history of trinitarian teaching has shaped the church and to discover the great freedom it brings to those who live with the God of the Bible in their minds and hearts.

I am thankful for the good people at Baker Publishing—Chad Allen, Jon Wilcox, and Anne Marie Miller—who helped edit the manuscript and make it what it is. I am grateful for Anne Marie's giftedness as a writer. Thanks to my friend Chris Ferebee for helping put the project together.

Special thanks to Paul Rhodes, who has been a spiritual director and mentor to me for many years. I am so grateful for the wisdom and care I have received from him.

I am grateful to the people of Imago Dei Community for continuing to live out of this vision of God and to risk themselves to announce it to the world. Thank you to my elders and fellow pastors for allowing me to serve with them. It is an amazing ride with lots of bumps, but God has us in his hands, and there is no better place to be.

As always, to my wife, Jeanne, and my kids, Josh, Kaylee, Zach, and Bryce. Without you there is no me. Our family has been God's gift to help me see the joy of being united to the Father, Son, and Spirit because he has given me the joy of being united to you.

Catch up with author
RICK MCKINLEY
▲▲▲

rickmckinley.net

🐦 @RickMcKinleypdx

f PastorRickMcKinley

imagodeicommunity.com